Workshop on Multilingual and Cross-lingual Methods in NLP 2016

Held at the 2016 Conference of the North American Chapter of the Association for Computational Linguistics: Human Language Technologies (NAACL HLT 2016)

San Diego, California, USA
17 June 2016

ISBN: 978-1-5108-2518-5

NAACL HLT 2016

Workshop on Multilingual and Cross-lingual Methods in NLP

Proceedings of the Workshop

June 17, 2016
San Diego, California, USA

We thank our sponsor Google Inc. for a generous support.

Introduction

The goal of this workshop is to expand the current area of cross-lingual learning to include more NLP problems, encourage approaches that explore low-resource scenarios, and improve upon existing approaches to multilinguality.

State-of-the-art NLP tools such as text parsing, speech recognition and synthesis, text and speech translation, semantic analysis and inference, rely on availability of language-specific data resources that exist only for a few resource-rich languages. To make NLP tools available in more languages, techniques have been developed for projecting such resources from resource-rich languages using parallel (translated) data as a bridge for cross-lingual NLP applications. The limiting reagent in these methods is parallel data or bilingual lexicons. While small parallel corpora do exist for many languages, suitably large parallel corpora are expensive, and these typically exist only for English and a few other geopolitically or economically important language pairs. Given this state of affairs, there is an urgent need for new cross-lingual methods, language-independent multilingual methods, and methods for establishing lexical links across languages that do not necessarily rely on large-scale parallel corpora. Without new strategies, most of the 7,000+ languages in the world—many with millions of speakers—will remain resource-poor from the standpoint of NLP.

This workshop features submissions from a diverse range of multilingual NLP problems, and invited talks from leading researchers working on multilingual NLP. We would like to thank the members of the program committee for their diligent work — the reviews were all very thorough, and detailed, which helped the authors improve their papers.

Organizers:

Dipanjan Das, Google Inc., USA
Chris Dyer, Google DeepMind, UK
Manaal Faruqui, Carnegie Mellon University, USA
Yulia Tsvetkov, Carnegie Mellon University, USA

Program Committee:

Waleed Ammar, Carnegie Mellon University, USA
Miguel Ballesteros, Pompeu Fabra, Spain
Mohit Bansal, Toyota Technological Institute at Chicago, USA
Phil Blunsom, Google DeepMind / Oxford, UK
Jan Botha, Google Inc., UK
Chris Callison-Burch, University of Pennsylvania, USA
Marine Carpuat, University of Maryland, USA
David Chiang, Notre Dame University, USA
Shay Cohen, University of Edinburgh, UK
Ryan Cotterell, Johns Hopkins University, USA
Rajarshi Das, University of Massachusetts, USA
Mona Diab, George Washington University, USA
Nadir Durrani, Qatar Computing Research Institute, Qatar
Kevin Gimpel, Toyota Technological Institute at Chicago, USA
Jiang Guo, Harbin Institute of Technology, China
David Hall, Semantic Machines, USA
Karl Moritz Hermann, Google DeepMind, UK
Dirk Hovy, University of Copenhagen, Denmark
Jagadeesh Jagarlamudi, Google Inc., USA
David Jurgens, Stanford University, USA
Young-Bum Kim, Microsoft Research, USA
Lingpeng Kong, Carnegie Mellon University, USA
Mirella Lapata, University of Edinburgh, UK
Omer Levy, Bar-Ilan University, Israel
Minh Thang Luong, Stanford University, USA
Ryan McDonald, Google Inc., UK
Gerard de Melo, Tsinghua University, China
Karthik Narasimhan, Massachusetts Institute of Technology, USA
Tahira Naseem, IBM Research, USA
Avneesh Saluja, AirBnb, USA
Anoop Sarkar, Simon Fraser University, Canada
Anders Søgaard, University of Copenhagen, Denmark
Oscar Tackstrom, Google Inc., USA
Jason Utt, University of Stuttgart, Germany

Shuly Wintner, University of Haifa, Israel
Dani Yogatama, Baidu, USA
Daniel Zeman, Charles University in Prague, Czech Republic

Invited Speakers:

Kyunghyun Cho, New York University, USA
Chris Dyer, Google DeepMind, UK
Dan Garrette, University of Washington, USA
Kevin Knight, University of Southern California, USA
Nathan Schneider, Georgetown University, USA
Ivan Titov, University of Amsterdam, Netherlands
David Yarowsky, Johns Hopkins University, USA

Table of Contents

Workshop Program

9:15–9:30   *Opening Remarks*
Yulia Tsvetkov

9:30–10:10   *Evaluation by Compression*
Invited Talk by Kevin Knight

10:10–10:50   *Multi-way, Multilingual Neural Machine Translation*
Invited Talk by Kyunghyun Cho

10:50–11:10   *Coffee Break*

11:10–11:50   *The Case for a Coarse-grained Multilingual Representation of Case and Adposition Semantics*
Invited Talk by Nathan Schneider

11:50–12:30   *To be decided*
Invited Talk by Chris Dyer

12:30–1:30   *Lunch and Setting Posters*

1:30–1:50   *Comparing Fifty Natural Languages and Twelve Genetic Languages Using Word Embedding Language Divergence (WELD) as a Quantitative Measure of Language Distance*
Ehsaneddin Asgari and Mohammad R.K. Mofrad

2:00–3:30   *Posters and Coffee*

3:30–4:10   *Cross-lingual and Unsupervised Learning of Semantic Representations*
Invited Talk by Ivan Titov

4:10–4:50   *Unsupervised Modeling of Code-Switching and Orthographic Variation, and its Application to the Study of Digital Humanities*
Invited Talk by Dan Garrette

4:50–5:30   *Cross-lingual Learning of Universalized Morphosemantics*
Invited Talk by David Yarowsky

5:30–5:45   *Best Paper & Poster Awards*

Learning Cross-lingual Representations with Matrix Factorization

Hanan Aldarmaki and **Mona Diab**
Department of Computer Science
The George Washington University
{aldarmaki;mtdiab}@gwu.edu

Abstract

We present a matrix factorization model for learning cross-lingual representations. Using sentence-aligned corpora, the proposed model learns distributed representations by factoring the given data into language-dependent factors and one shared factor. Moreover, the model can quickly learn shared representations for more than two languages without undermining the quality of the monolingual components. The model achieves an accuracy of 88% on English to German cross-lingual document classification, and 0.8 Pearson correlation on Spanish-English cross-lingual semantic textual similarity. While the results do not beat state-of-the-art performance in these tasks, we show that the crosslingual models are at least as good as their monolingual counterparts.

1 Introduction

A large body of NLP research in recent years has focused on representing natural language words and phrases in high-dimensional continuous vector spaces. Such representations can be integrated with various NLP applications as they can be easily learned, processed, and compared, often in an unsupervised or semi-supervised manner. Distributed representations of words, or word embeddings, can be learned using global word co-occurrence statistics as in matrix factorization models (Guo and Diab, 2012; Pennington et al., 2014), or using local context as in neural probabilistic language models (Bengio et al., 2003; Collobert and Weston, 2008; Socher et al., 2013). Compared to word embeddings, representing variable-length sequences using a vector space model is more challenging since these vectors need to encode complex semantic structures and relationships. Several models have been proposed for learning phrase and sentence embeddings, either by combining word embeddings (Klementiev et al., 2012) or directly learning the sentence representations (Le and Mikolov, 2014).

In our global world of information, many NLP problems exist in multilingual and cross-lingual settings. It is often desirable to generalize sentence representations to several languages such that sentences conveying the same meaning in any language are clustered together and potentially mapped to one another in the semantic space. Such cross-lingual representations can then be used directly in NLP applications such as machine translation and cross-lingual question answering. They can also be used to learn classifiers that generalize to languages beyond the ones used in training.

A number of models have recently been proposed for learning cross-lingual compositional representations (Klementiev et al., 2012; Shi et al., 2015; Pennington et al., 2014; Cavallanti et al., 2010; Mikolov et al., 2013; Coulmance et al., 2015; Pham et al., 2015). We propose a relatively simple and nuanced model inspired by the monolingual weighted matrix factorization (WMF) model proposed in (Guo and Diab, 2012), which we extend to the cross-lingual setting.

The WMF model learns word representations by decomposing a sparse tf-idf matrix into two low-rank factor matrices representing words and sen-

1

Proceedings of the Workshop on Multilingual and Cross-lingual Methods in NLP, pages 1–9,
San Diego, California, June 17, 2016. ©2016 Association for Computational Linguistics

tences. The weights are adjusted to reflect the confidence levels in reconstructing observed vs. missing words in the original matrix. Representations for variable-length sequences can be calculated by minimizing the reconstruction error as described in Section 2.1. In this paper, we propose to extend this model to the cross-lingual setting by modeling two languages in parallel to obtain shared semantic representations. The proposed model has a simple loss function and only uses sentence-aligned data for learning the shared representations. Furthermore, the model can be readily extended to multiple languages without loss of quality. We describe the model in two variations in Section 2.2.

We evaluate the quality of these representations using the cross-lingual document classification task, where a multi-class perceptron is trained to classify documents into four categories. Using German and English labeled short documents, the classifier is trained on one language and tested on the other. Using the compositional representations generated by our model, we achieve an accuracy of 88% in the English→German classification task. We also evaluate on the Semeval cross-lingual semantic textual similarity (STS) task, where we assign a similarity score to pairs of English and Spanish sentences. Our model yields a performance of 0.8 Pearson correlation in this task.

2 Proposed Approach

Word co-occurrence statistics and matrix factorization can be exploited to learn latent semantic representations for words, sentences, and documents (Pennington et al., 2014; Guo and Diab, 2012). We focus on one such model, the weighted matrix factorization model proposed in (Guo and Diab, 2012), as a basis for our crosslingual representations, which is described in the following section. Similar extensions can be implemented for other matrix factorizaiton mehtods.

2.1 Background: Weighted Matrix Factorization (WMF)

In the WMF model proposed in (Guo and Diab, 2012), a large corpus is represented as an $m \times n$ matrix X, where each X_{ij} cell is the tf-idf weight of word i in sentence j. This sparse matrix is then factorized into a $k \times m$ matrix P and a $k \times n$ matrix Q, such that $X = P^T Q$. The factorization results in k-dimensional representations for words and sentences: the columns in P are latent k-dimensional representations for words, and the columns in Q are latent k-dimensional representations for the training sentences.

The values of P and Q can be calculated by minimizing the following weighted loss function:

$$C = \sum_{i,j} W_{ij}(P_{:,i}^T Q_{:,j} - X_{ij})^2 + \lambda(\|P\|^2 + \|Q\|^2) \quad (1)$$

where λ is a regularization parameter to avoid overfitting, and W is an $m \times n$ weight matrix. The weights reflect the confidence levels associated with the reconstruction errors of the corresponding items in X. A small weight is assigned to all missing words, ($X_{ij} = 0$), to reflect an appropriate level of uncertainty:

$$W_{i,j} = \begin{cases} 1, & \text{if } X_{i,j} \neq 0 \\ w_m, & \text{if } X_{i,j} = 0 \end{cases}$$

where $w_m << 1$ is a fixed weight that is determined empirically; In other words, we assign minimal confidence that each word in the vocabulary could legitimately correlate with any given sentence, while the confidence level is highest for observed words. Using this weighted scheme is explained in more details and experimentally justified in (Guo and Diab, 2012).

By fixing P, the cost function becomes quadratic in Q and the global minimum is achieved using the matrix Q_{min} that satisfies $C'(Q_{min}) = 0$. The jth column in Q_{min} is calculated as follows:

$$Q_{:,j} = (PW^j P^T + \lambda I)^{-1} PW^j X_{:,j} \quad (2)$$

where W^j is a diagonal matrix with coefficients W_{ij} in row/column j (the jth column of W).

Similarly, the vectors in P_{min} are calculated by fixing Q and minimizing the cost function $P(Q)$:

$$P_{:,i} = (QW^i Q^T + \lambda I)^{-1} QW^i X_{i,:} \quad (3)$$

where W^i is a diagonal matrix with coefficients W_{ij} in row/column i (the ith row of W).

Thus, alternating least squares is used to minimize $C(P, Q)$ by iteratively fixing P to calculate Q, then fixing Q to calculate P using equations (2) and (3). Note that these calculations can be done in parallel and the sparsity of the original matrix can be exploited for a more efficient computation of vectors.[1]

To generate vector representations for additional sentences after training, P is fixed and Q is calculated for the new sentences using equation (2). In other words, we calculate the representations that minimize the loss function (1), which is quadratic when P is fixed.

2.2 Cross-lingual Extensions to WMF

Here we describe our proposed extension of the WMF model for learning bilingual semantic representations. Given a parallel corpus of n sentence pairs, we generate an $m \times n$ tf-idf matrix X for the first language, and an $l \times n$ tf-idf matrix Y for the second language, where m and l are the number of words in the vocabulary of each language. The learning objective of the bilingual WMF model is to factorize both X and Y into two language-specific factors and one shared factor. More precisely, the desired factorization would result in a $k \times m$ matrix P, a $k \times l$ matrix A, and a $k \times n$ matrix Q, such that $X = P^T Q$ and $Y = A^T Q$. To achieve these bilingual objectives, we define two methods for calculating the loss function for both languages as detailed below: A global bilingual loss function (BMF), and a monolingual loss function with an explicit crosslingual factor (CMF).

2.2.1 BMF: Bilingual Matrix Factorization

We define a global loss function for both languages as follows:

$$C = \sum_{i,j} W_{ij}(P_{:,i}^T Q_{:,j} - X_{ij})^2 + \sum_{d,j} U_{dj}(A_{:,d}^T Q_{:,j} - Y_{dj})^2$$
$$+ \lambda(\|P\|^2 + \|Q\|^2 + \|A\|^2) \quad (4)$$

where U *is the weight matrix for* Y*, defined similarly to* W*.*

This objective function is convex if we fix two of the factor matrices and minimize with respect to the remaining factor. Alternating least squares can be used to estimate the factors iteratively using the following three equations:

$$Q_{:,j} = (PW^j P^T + AU^j A^T + \lambda I)^{-1}(PW^j X_j + AU^j Y_{:,j})$$
$$P_{:,i} = (QW^i Q^T + \lambda I)^{-1} QW^i X_{i,:}$$
$$A_{:,d} = (QU^d Q^T + \lambda I)^{-1} QU^d Y_{d,:}$$
$$(5)$$

To generate vector representations for additional sentences in either language, the language-specific factors P and A are fixed, and the semantic vectors $Q_{:,j}$ are calculated using equation (2) for language 1 and equation (6) for language 2.

$$Q_{:,j} = (AU^j A^T + \lambda I)^{-1} AU^j Y_{:,j} \quad (6)$$

In other words, the two models are independent once the training is complete, but the resultant representations are expected to reflect shared semantic components.

2.2.2 CMF: Crosslingual Matrix Factorization

Alternatively, we can define two loss functions with a shared crosslingual factor:

$$C_1 = \sum_{i,j} W_{ij}(P_{:,i}^T Q_{:,j} - X_{ij})^2 + \lambda(\|P\|^2 + \|Q\|^2)$$
$$C_2 = \sum_{d,j} U_{dj}(A_{:,d}^T Q_{:,j} - Y_{dj})^2 + \lambda(\|A\|^2 + \|Q\|^2)$$
$$(7)$$

Minimizing C_1 and C_2 separately is equivalent to training two separate monolingual models. To achieve the bilingual objective, we train only C_1 as a monolingual model, then use the learned factors P to find A. If we assume that the compositional representations generated by P are optimal, then we can use it to fix Q in C_2, and the loss function becomes quadratic in A; all we have to do is find the values of A that minimize C_2.

The training procedure is carried out as follows:

1. Independently train a monolingual WMF model for a pivot language.

2. Using a parallel corpus and the trained word representations P for the pivot language, generate sentence representations Q using equation (2)

3. Using the same parallel corpus, and fixing Q as calculated in step 2, calculate word representations A for the second language using equation (5).

This method can be readily extended to more than two languages. Using one trained monolingual model, we can quickly learn representations for any number of languages using sentence-aligned data.

3   Related Work

The weighted matrix factorization model we extend was first proposed in (Guo and Diab, 2012) to learn distributed vector representations for words in the monolingual setting. These vectors are then used to generate distributed representations for variable-length sequences by minimizing the reconstruction error. The GloVe algorithm proposed (Pennington et al., 2014) is also a weighted matrix factorization method, but it includes additional word-specific bias terms and uses a different weighting scheme.

As mentioned above, we extend the WMF model proposed in (Guo and Diab, 2012) to bilingual and multilingual settings by forcing the two monolingual components to use a shared factor. (Shi et al., 2015) proposes a similar approach for learning bilingual embeddings. They extend GloVe (Pennington et al., 2014) to the bilingual case using a matrix of bilingual co-occurrence counts with word alignments in addition to the monolingual components. They also propose an alternative method of minimizing the Euclidean distance between words that may be translations of one another. This model is similar in spirit to our model, but it has a different objective function that incorporates cross-lingual co-occurrence statistics or word alignments. Extending that model to more than two languages has not been studied.

In general, several models have been proposed recently to learn cross-lingual semantic representations. Most proposed models learn cross-lingual word embeddings and use them to compose representations for variable-length sequences. For example, (Klementiev et al., 2012) uses a multi-task learning objective (Cavallanti et al., 2010) to align word embeddings for multiple languages. Sentence representations are then composed using idf-weighted sum of word representations. In (Mikolov et al., 2013), word embeddings are first learned sep-

arately for each language, and then a linear mapping is learned between the source and target languages.

The `Trans-gram` model introduced in (Coulmance et al., 2015) learns shared representations of several languages efficiently using English as a pivot language. This is comparable to our model in speed and flexibility in learning several language representations. However, the `Trans-gram` model only learns word embeddings, and sentence representations are calculated using idf-weighted average of word embeddings. On the other hand, the WMF model generates sentence representations by minimizing the data reconstruction error in addition to the word embeddings that can be used to calculate an idf-weighted average.

In (Pham et al., 2015), distributed representations for bilingual phrases and sentences are learned using an extended version of the paragraph vector model described in (Le and Mikolov, 2014) by forcing parallel sentences to share one vector. This model learns shared sentence representations directly and achieves state-of-the-art performance in the document classification task.

4   Empirical Evaluation

We evaluate our crosslingual models in two empirical evaluation settings: Crosslingual Semantic Textual Similarity (STS), and Cross-lingual Document Classification (CLDC).

4.1   Data

Monolingual Data: For the monolingual English model, the training set consists of 700K sentences derived from various resources. We extract and combine the following sets: a random set of 150K sentences from LDC's English Gigaword fifth edition (Parker et al., 2011), a random set of 150K sentences from the English Wikipedia[2], the Brown Corpus (Francis, 1964), Wordnet (Miller, 1995) and Wiktionary[3] definitions appended with examples.

Bilingual Data: We extract training data for the bilingual models from WMT13 (Macháček and Bojar, 2013) sentence-aligned parallel corpora, specifically version 7 of the EuroParl parallel corpus (Koehn, 2005), the multiUN parallel corpus (Eisele

---

[2]http://en.wikipedia.org
[3]http://www.wiktionary.org

and Chen, 2010), and news commentary data for two language pairs: English-Spanish (en-es) and English-German (en-de). We train each bilingual model using a sample of 1M sentence pairs from these datasets.

All sentences in our data are tokenized and stemmed, and number sequences are replaced with a special token as a normalization step. We use the Stanford CoreNLP toolkit (Manning et al., 2014) for English preprocessing, and Treetagger tools (Schmid, 1995) for both Spanish and German data. Words that appear less than 5 times in the training set are discarded from the vocabulary. The final vocabulary sizes for each model are shown below:

Monolingual English	55,881
English from the en-es set	25,057
English from the en-de set	21,879
Spanish	30,411
German	57,431

4.2 Parameter settings for empirical tasks

We train our bilingual BMF models strictly using the bilingual parallel data. On the other hand, we train the English pivot model used in CMF strictly using the English monolingual data, while the parallel corpora are only used for training the Spanish and German components of the CMF models. For the BMF models and the English monolingual model, we run the alternating least squares (ALS) algorithm for 20 iterations. We use the following parameters for all models: k=300, $w_m = 0.01$ and $\lambda = 20$.[4]

4.3 Using English as a Pivot: Cross-lingual STS Validation

One of the advantages of the CMF model is that it can be readily used to learn representations for several languages. We test this hypothesis by using English as a pivot language to learn cross-lingual correspondences between German and Spanish. Hence in this setting, we only use the English model to factor both the Spanish and German models independently, but we assume that any two learned models are directly comparable. Accordingly, WMT12 (Callison-Burch et al., 2012) news test set is used as a validation set to verify that the models actually map the

Dataset	en-es	en-de	de-es
Parallel	0.65	0.60	*0.62*
Random	0.11	0.11	0.10

Table 1: Average semantic similarity between sentence pairs using WMT12 test set

cross-lingual sentences into a shared semantic space. Table 1 shows the average cosine similarity between parallel pairs in the validation set, and the average similarity between a random permutation of the set.

These results indicate that the models learn to distinguish between similar and dissimilar sentences since the parallel sentences have much higher cosine similarity than random pairs. We also observe an equivalent performance for the Spanish-German sentences, even though we do not directly train a model for this language pair.

4.4 Cross-lingual Semantic Textual Similarity

Semantic Textual Similarity (STS) is a measure of the degree of similarity between two sentences. STS scores range from 0 to 5, where higher values indicate closer semantic content. Cross-lingual STS measures the degree of similarity between sentences from two different languages.

Using the BMF and CMF cross-lingual models, we generate sentence vectors for the given pairs, then we calculate the cosine similarity between each pair. Since most of the output is positive, and negative values are generally very close to zero, we round up negative similarity values to 0. We then convert the values from the [0-1] range to the [0-5] range by multiplying the scores by 5 [5].

Table 2 shows the results on the test data of Semeval 2016 en-es cross-lingual STS shared task. The evaluation metric is the Pearson Correlation Coefficient. The CMF models perform better than BMF in this task. We also show the results of the official Semeval first rank system, UWB.

4.5 Monolingual Evaluation

We evaluate the performance of the monolingual components learned using BMF or CMF models on the Semeval monolingual Spanish semantic textual similarity (STS) task, namely STS 2014 and STS

---

[4]These parameters are tuned empirically and we found these values to be robust across models.

[5]Note that this scaling operation does not affect the evaluation results, but we do it for consistency.

Model	News	Multi Source	Mean
BMF	0.83	0.72	0.78
CMF	0.87	0.73	0.80
UWB	0.91	0.82	0.86

Table 2: Cross-lingual STS EN-SP Test results using Pearson Correlation Coefficient.

Model	WK14	NW14	WK15	NW15
Semeval Best	0.78	0.82	0.71	0.68
WMF*	0.77	0.83	0.64	0.55
mono WMF	0.67	0.80	0.46	0.55
BMF	0.69	0.80	0.50	0.51
CMF	0.70	0.83	0.53	0.52

Table 3: Performance on STS 2014 (WK14, NW14) and STS 2015 (WK15, NW15) test sets for monolingual Spanish STS task

2015. The objective of this evaluation is to check whether the quality is hurt by forcing the factors into a shared semantic space. We train two monolingual models:

Mono WMF: We train a monolingual Spanish WMF model using the Spanish component of the parallel training set, which consists of 1M sentences. This is the same set used to train the cross-lingual models, so the results are comparable.

WMF*: We train another Spanish WMF model with a more varied training set, similar in construction to the English monolingual model. This training set includes Wikipedia and newswire articles, so it's more similar to the test set. This set consists of about 400K sentences extracted from the second edition of Spanish Gigawords (Mendona et al., 2009) and the Spanish Wikipedia Corpus (Reese et al., 2010).

We use the same values for all the parameters, and we run ALS for 20 iterations. Table 3 shows the results on Semeval Spanish STS 2014 dataset (Agirre et al., 2014), which includes sentence pairs extracted from Spanish Wikipedia and news articles. We also show the results on the harder 2015 dataset (Agirre et al., 2015), which intentionally includes sentence pairs with higher degree of difficulty, such as sentences with shared vocabulary but different compositional meaning. The first row depicts the results obtained by the top system participating in the Semeval task, Semeval Best.

While none of our models outperforms the official Semeval top ranking system, Semeval Best, we show that the Spanish models trained using the BMF and CMF models actually outperform the monolingual Spanish model (mono-WMF) when we use the same dataset for training. The advantage of a monolingual model, however, is that it can be trained using more

Model	Vector size	en→de	de→en
Maj-Class	40	46.8	46.8
Multi-task	40	77.6	71.1
CLSim	40	92.7	80.2
Trans-gram	100	87.8	78.7
Trans-gram	300	91.1	78.4
BMF	300	88.6	68.9
CMF	300	88.2	70.7
para-doc	500	92.7	91.5

Table 4: Cross-lingual document classification accuracy

varied training data, as evident by the higher performance of WMF ⋆, outperforming our cross-lingual derived models.

4.6 Cross-lingual Document Classification (CLDC)

The cross-lingual document classification (CLDC) task introduced in (Klementiev et al., 2012) is a supervised task used to evaluate cross-lingual representations in short document classification. The training and test sets are news stories extracted from the English and German sections of the Reuters multilingual corpus (Lewis et al., 2004). The documents are classified into four categories/topics: C (Corporate/Industrial), E (Economics), G (Government/Social), and M (Markets). For each language, a set of 1K documents is used to train a multi-class Perceptron classifier, and a set of 5K documents is used to test the classifier. For the purpose of evaluating the cross-lingual representations, the classifier is trained on one language and tested on

	to en	to de
from en	88.5	88.2
from de	93.7	70.7

Table 5: Document classification accuracy for CMF model

the other. Thus, we evaluate our models in the English to German direction (en→de), where the model is trained to classify English documents and tested by classifying German documents, and vice versa (de→en).

We generate document representations directly by concatenating all the sentences in each document and using the BMF and CMF models to generate 300-dimensional vectors for each document. The results are shown in Table 4. We show the results of the original `Majority-class` and `Multitask` baselines as listed in (Klementiev et al., 2012). Furthermore, we show the results of several competitive systems on the CLDC task, namely: the `Trans-gram` model (Coulmance et al., 2015), the cross-lingual matrix co-factorization `CLSim` model proposed in (Shi et al., 2015), and the state-of-the art performance by `para-doc` as described in (Pham et al., 2015). We also report the size of the document vector representations for each model.

We note that the performance on the en→de significantly outperforms the other direction of de→en. This trend is apparent in all other models except for `para-doc`. This asymmetry in performance is likely a result of the bag-of-words approach which doesn't account for word ordering. The performance in both directions is lower than that of the competing models, especially in the de→en direction. Also, as shown in table 5, the performance in the crosslingual en→de setting is at least as good as the performamance in the monolingual en→en setting, while the performance of the de→en crosslingual setting is much lower than the monolingual de→de setting. This indicates that some of the dimensions are not transferred from the German to the English vectors, possible due to unmatched vocabulary cause by the multitude of compound words in German.

5   Discussion and Conclusions

We proposed a new approach for generating cross-lingual semantic representations for variable-length sequences using weighted matrix factorization models. These models generally achieved good results in the cross-lingual document classification and cross-lingual semantic similarity tasks. One limiting characteristic of the proposed models is the need to use sentence-aligned data, which could undermine the performance in textual domains that lack parallel resources. This can be remedied to some extent by using more representative data in training the pivot model.

A valuable feature of the proposed model is the possibility to learn shared representations for an unlimited number of languages as long as we have sentence-aligned data with one of the learned languages. Training additional languages is trivial since the additional factors are calculated deterministically and independently. In other words, we can learn representations for each language separately and without the need to retrain the available models. Moreover, the model is simple and robust as we learned good representations using relatively small parallel datasets and without parameter optimization. In addition, the monolingual components of the cross-lingual models are as good as, if not better than, the monolingual models learned independently using the same training data. These results direct our attention to the monolingual models we started with; the performance of the crosslingual models is simply a reflection of the quality of the monolingual models they are based on. We focus on improving the monlingual weighted matrix factorization model in future work.

References

Eneko Agirre, Carmen Banea, Claire Cardie, Daniel Cer, Mona Diab, Aitor Gonzalez-Agirre, Weiwei Guo, Rada Mihalcea, German Rigau, and Janyce Wiebe. 2014. Semeval-2014 task 10: Multilingual semantic textual similarity. In *Proceedings of the 8th International Workshop on Semantic Evaluation (SemEval 2014)*, pages 81–91, Dublin, Ireland, August. Association for Computational Linguistics and Dublin City University.

Eneko Agirre, Carmen Banea, Claire Cardie, Daniel Cer, Mona Diab, Aitor Gonzalez-Agirre, Weiwei Guo, Inigo Lopez-Gazpio, Montse Maritxalar, Rada Mihalcea, German Rigau, Larraitz Uria, and Janyce Wiebe. 2015. Semeval-2015 task 2: Semantic textual similarity, english, spanish and pilot on interpretability. In *Proceedings of the 9th International Workshop on Semantic Evaluation (SemEval 2015)*, pages 252–263, Denver, Colorado, June. Association for Computational Linguistics.

Yoshua Bengio, Réjean Ducharme, Pascal Vincent, and

Christian Janvin. 2003. A neural probabilistic language model. *J. Mach. Learn. Res.*, 3:1137–1155, March.

Chris Callison-Burch, Philipp Koehn, Christof Monz, Matt Post, Radu Soricut, and Lucia Specia. 2012. Findings of the 2012 workshop on statistical machine translation. In *Proceedings of the Seventh Workshop on Statistical Machine Translation*, pages 10–51, Montréal, Canada, June. Association for Computational Linguistics.

Giovanni Cavallanti, Nicol Cesa-Bianchi, and Claudio Gentile. 2010. Linear algorithms for online multitask classification. *Journal of Machine Learning Research*, 11:2901–2934.

Ronan Collobert and Jason Weston. 2008. A unified architecture for natural language processing: Deep neural networks with multitask learning. In *Proceedings of the 25th International Conference on Machine Learning*, ICML '08, pages 160–167, New York, NY, USA. ACM.

Jocelyn Coulmance, Jean-Marc Marty, Guillaume Wenzek, and Amine Benhalloum. 2015. Trans-gram, fast crosslingual word embeddings. *Proceedings of the 2015 Conference on Empirical Methods in Natural Language Processing*, pages 1109–1113.

Andreas Eisele and Yu Chen. 2010. Multiun: A multilingual corpus from united nation documents. In Daniel Tapias, Mike Rosner, Stelios Piperidis, Jan Odjik, Joseph Mariani, Bente Maegaard, Khalid Choukri, and Nicoletta Calzolari (Conference Chair), editors, *Proceedings of the Seventh conference on International Language Resources and Evaluation*, pages 2868–2872. European Language Resources Association (ELRA), 5.

W. Nelson Francis. 1964. A standard sample of present-day english for use with digital computers. *Report to the U.S. Office of Education on Cooperative Research Project No. E-007.*

Weiwei Guo and Mona Diab. 2012. Modeling sentences in the latent space. In *Proceedings of the 50th Annual Meeting of the Association for Computational Linguistics: Long Papers - Volume 1*, ACL '12, pages 864–872, Stroudsburg, PA, USA. Association for Computational Linguistics.

Yifan Hu, Yehuda Koren, and Chris Volinsky. 2008. Collaborative filtering for implicit feedback datasets. In *Proceedings of the 2008 Eighth IEEE International Conference on Data Mining*, ICDM '08, pages 263–272, Washington, DC, USA. IEEE Computer Society.

Alexandre Klementiev, Ivan Titov, and Binod Bhattarai. 2012. Inducing crosslingual distributed representations of words.

Philipp Koehn. 2005. Europarl: A Parallel Corpus for Statistical Machine Translation. In *Conference Proceedings: the tenth Machine Translation Summit*, pages 79–86, Phuket, Thailand. AAMT, AAMT.

Quoc Le and Tomas Mikolov. 2014. Distributed representations of sentences and documents. In Tony Jebara and Eric P. Xing, editors, *Proceedings of the 31st International Conference on Machine Learning (ICML-14)*, pages 1188–1196. JMLR Workshop and Conference Proceedings.

David D. Lewis, Yiming Yang, Tony G. Rose, and Fan Li. 2004. Rcv1: A new benchmark collection for text categorization research. *J. Mach. Learn. Res.*, 5:361–397, December.

Matouš Macháček and Ondřej Bojar. 2013. Results of the WMT13 metrics shared task. In *Proceedings of the Eighth Workshop on Statistical Machine Translation*, pages 45–51, Sofia, Bulgaria, August. Association for Computational Linguistics.

Christopher D. Manning, Mihai Surdeanu, John Bauer, Jenny Finkel, Steven J. Bethard, and David McClosky. 2014. The Stanford CoreNLP natural language processing toolkit. In *Association for Computational Linguistics (ACL) System Demonstrations*, pages 55–60.

Angelo Mendona, David Graff, and Denise DiPersio. 2009. Spanish gigaword second edition ldc2009t21. *Web download file.*

Tomas Mikolov, Quoc V. Le, and Ilya Sutskever. 2013. Exploiting similarities among languages for machine translation. *CoRR.*

George A. Miller. 1995. Wordnet: A lexical database for english. *Commun. ACM*, 38(11):39–41, November.

Robert Parker, David Graff, Junbo Kong, Ke Chen, and Kazuaki Maeda. 2011. English gigaword fifth edition ldc2011t07. *Web download file.*

Jeffrey Pennington, Richard Socher, and Christopher D. Manning. 2014. Glove: Global vectors for word representation. In *Proceedings of the 2014 Conference on Empirical Methods in Natural Language Processing (EMNLP 2014)*, pages 1532–1543.

Hieu Pham, Thang Luong, and Christopher Manning. 2015. Learning distributed representations for multilingual text sequences. *NAACL.*

Samuel Reese, Gemma Boleda Torrent, Montserrat Cuadros Oller, Lluís Padró, and German Rigau Claramunt. 2010. Word-sense disambiguated multilingual wikipedia corpus. In *7th International Conference on Language Resources and Evaluation.*

Helmut Schmid. 1995. Treetagger— a language independent part-of-speech tagger. *Institut für Maschinelle Sprachverarbeitung, Universität Stuttgart*, 43:28.

Tianze Shi, Zhiyuan Liu, Yang Liu, and Maosong Sun. 2015. Learning cross-lingual word embeddings via matrix co-factorization. In *Proceedings of the 53rd Annual Meeting of the Association for Computational*

Linguistics and the 7th International Joint Conference on Natural Language Processing (Volume 2: Short Papers), pages 567–572, Beijing, China, July. Association for Computational Linguistics.

Richard Socher, John Bauer, Christopher D. Manning, and Andrew Y. Ng. 2013. Parsing With Compositional Vector Grammars. In *ACL*.

Should Have, Would Have, Could Have

Investigating Verb Group Representations for Parsing with Universal Dependencies

Miryam de Lhoneux and **Joakim Nivre**
Uppsala University
Department of Linguistics and Philology
{miryam.de_lhoneux, joakim.nivre}@lingfil.uu.se

Abstract

Treebanks have recently been released for a number of languages with the harmonized annotation created by the Universal Dependencies project. The representation of certain constructions in UD are known to be suboptimal for parsing and may be worth transforming for the purpose of parsing. In this paper, we focus on the representation of verb groups. Several studies have shown that parsing works better when auxiliaries are the head of auxiliary dependency relations which is not the case in UD. We therefore transformed verb groups in UD treebanks, parsed the test set and transformed it back, and contrary to expectations, observed significant decreases in accuracy. We provide suggestive evidence that improvements in previous studies were obtained because the transformation helps disambiguating POS tags of main verbs and auxiliaries. The question of why parsing accuracy decreases with this approach in the case of UD is left open.

1 Introduction

Universal Dependencies[1] (henceforth UD) (Nivre, 2015) is a recent project that is attempting to harmonize syntactic annotation in dependency treebanks across languages. This is done through the development of annotation guidelines. Some guidelines have been hypothesized to be suboptimal for parsing. In the literature, certain representations of certain constructions have been shown to be better

---

[1] http://universaldependencies.github.io/docs/

than their alternatives for parsing, for example in Schwartz et al. (2012). The UD guidelines however have been written with the intent to maximize cross-linguistic parallelism and this constraint has forced the guidelines developers to sometimes choose representations that are known to be worse for parsing (de Marneffe et al., 2014). For that reason, de Marneffe et al. (2014) suggest that those representations could be modified for the purpose of parsing, thus creating a *parsing representation*. Transforming tree representations for the purpose of parsing is not a new idea. It has been done for constituency parsing for example by Collins (1999) but also for dependency parsing for example by Nilsson et al. (2007). Nilsson et al. (2007) modified the representation of several constructions in several languages and obtained a consistent improvement in parsing accuracy. In this paper, we will investigate the case of the verb group construction and attempt to reproduce the study by Nilsson et al. (2007) on UD treebanks to find out whether or not the alternative representation is useful for parsing with UD.

2 Background

2.1 Tree Transformations for Parsing

Nilsson et al. (2006) have shown that modifying coordination constructions and verb groups from their representation in the Prague Dependency Treebank (henceforth PDT) to a representation described in Melčuk (1988) (Mel'čuk style, henceforth MS) improves dependency parsing for Czech. The procedure they follow is as follows:

1. Transform the training data.

Proceedings of the Workshop on Multilingual and Cross-lingual Methods in NLP, pages 10–19,
San Diego, California, June 17, 2016. ©2016 Association for Computational Linguistics

2. Train a model on that transformed data.

3. Parse the test data.

4. Transform the parsed data back to the original representation (for comparison with the original gold standard).

Nilsson et al. (2007) have shown that these same modifications as well as the modification of non-projective structures helps parsing in four languages. Schwartz et al. (2012) conducted a study over the alternative representations of 6 constructions across 5 parsing models for English and found that some of them are easier to parse than others. Their results were consistent across parsing models.

The motivations behind those two types of studies are different. Nilsson et al. (2006) have originally a representation that is more semantically oriented and potentially useful for NLP applications which they therefore wish their output to have, the PDT style, and change it to a representation that is more syntactically oriented, the MS style, because it is easier to parse. By contrast, Schwartz et al. (2012) have no a priori preference for any of the different alternatives of the constructions they study and instead study the effect of the different representations on parsing for the purpose of choosing one representation over the other. Their methodology is therefore different, they evaluate the different representations on their respective gold standard. They argue that accuracy within a representation is a good indicator of the learnability of that representation and they argue that learnability is a good criterion for selecting a syntactic representation among alternatives. In any case, these studies seem to show that such transformations can affect parsing for various languages and for various parsing models.

Silveira and Manning (2015) were the first to obtain negative results from such transformations. They attempted to modify certain constructions in a UD treebank to improve parsing for English but failed to show any improvement. Some transformations even decreased parsing accuracy. They observe that when they transform their parsed data back to the original representation, they can amplify parser errors. As a matter of fact, a transformation can be prompted by the presence of only one dependency relation but involve transformations of many

surrounding dependency relations. The verb group transformation is such an example and will be described in section 3. If, then, a wrong dependency relation prompts a transformation in the parsed data, its surrounding items which might have been correct become wrong. A wrong parse can then become worse. They take this as partial explanation for the results that are inconsistent with the literature. However, the same problem can have arisen in Nilsson et al. (2006) and may have downplayed the effects that those studies have observed. It therefore seems that this explanation is not enough to account for those results.

This raises the question of whether this phenomenon actually happened in the study by Nilsson et al. (2007). It would be interesting to know if the effects they observed were affected by this kind of error amplification. It seems that there is still a lot to do to study the impact of different representations on parsing with UD as well as on dependency parsing more generally. We propose to take one step in that direction in this paper.

2.2 Error Analysis for Dependency Parsing

McDonald and Nivre (2007) conducted an extensive error analysis on two parsers in order to compare them. They compare the effect of sentence length on the two models, the effect of the structure of the graph (i.e. how close to the root individual arcs are) on the two models as well as the accuracy of the models on different POS tags and on different dependency relations. These comparisons allow them to provide insights into the strengths and weaknesses of each model. Conducting such an error analysis that compares baseline models with their transformed version could provide some further insights into the effects obtained with tree transformations. Attempting such a detailed error analysis is beyond the scope of this project but some steps will be taken in that direction and are described in Section 4.

2.3 Verb Groups

In the PDT, main verbs are the head of auxiliary dependencies, as in Figure 1. Nilsson et al. (2007) show that making the auxiliary the head of the dependency as in Figure 2 is useful for parsing Czech and Slovenian.

Schwartz et al. (2012) also report that, in English,

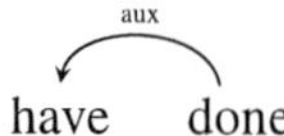

Figure 1: PDT representation of verb groups

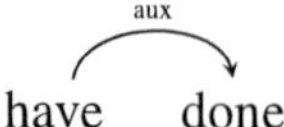

Figure 2: MS representation of verb groups

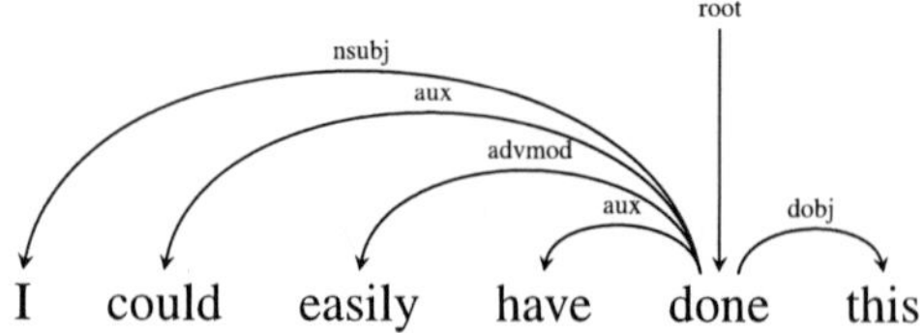

Figure 3: Example (1) annotated in UD style

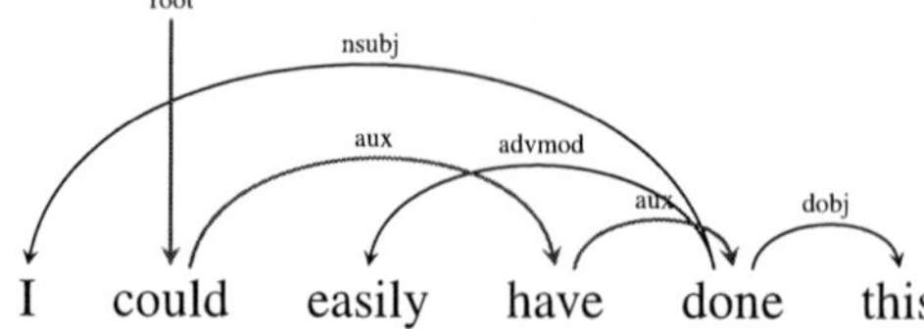

Figure 4: Intermediate representation between UD and MS of Example (1). Thick blue dependencies are those that changed compared to Figure 3.

verb groups are easier to parse when the auxiliary is the head (as in PDT) than when the verb is the head (as in MS). Since UD adopts the PDT style representation of verb groups, it would be interesting to find out whether or not transforming them to MS could also improve parsing. This is what will be attempted in this study.

Nilsson et al. (2006) describe algorithms for such a transformation as well as its back transformation. However, their back transformation algorithm assumes that the auxiliary appears to the left of the verb which is not always the case. In addition, it is unclear what they do with the cases in which there are two auxiliaries in a verb group. For these reasons, we will use a slightly modified version of this algorithm that we describe in Section 3.

3 Methodology

3.1 General Approach

We will follow the methodology from Nilsson et al. (2007), that is, to transform, parse and then detransform the data so as to compare the original and the transformed model on the original gold standard. The method from Schwartz et al. (2012) which consists in comparing the baseline and the transformed data on their respective gold standard is less relevant here because UD is believed to be a useful representation and that the aim will be to improve parsing within that representation. However, as was argued in that study, their method can give an indication of the learnability of a construction and can potentially be used to understand the results obtained by the parse-transform-detransform method. For this reason, this method will also be attempted. In addition, the original parsed data will also be transformed into the MS gold standard for comparison with the MS parsed data on the MS gold standard. Comparing

the two can potentially help find out if the error amplifications described in the background section are strongly influencing the results. As a matter of fact, if the transformed model is penalized by error amplifications on the original gold standard, it is expected that the original model will be penalized in the same way on the transformed gold standard.

3.2 Transformation Algorithm

The transformation algorithm is illustrated by Figures 3, 4 and 5 which represent the transformation of a sentence with a verb group given in Example (1). Figure 3 is the original UD representation of this example, Figure 4, an intermediate representation and Figure 5 is the final MS representation.

(1)   I could easily have done this

The transformation first looks for verb groups in a dependency graph. Those verb groups are collected in the set V. A verb group V_i has a main verb $V_{i_{mv}}$ (*done* in the example) and a set of auxiliaries $V_{i_{aux}}$ with at least one element (*could* and *have* in the example). Verb groups are collected by traversing the sentence from left to right, looking at auxiliary dependency relations. An auxiliary dependency relation $w_{aux} \xleftarrow{aux} w_{mv}$ is a relation where the main verb is the head and the auxiliary is the dependent. Only auxiliary dependency relations between two verbal forms are considered. When such a dependency relation is found, if there is a V_i in V that has the head of the dependency relation (w_{mv}) as main verb $V_{i_{mv}}$,

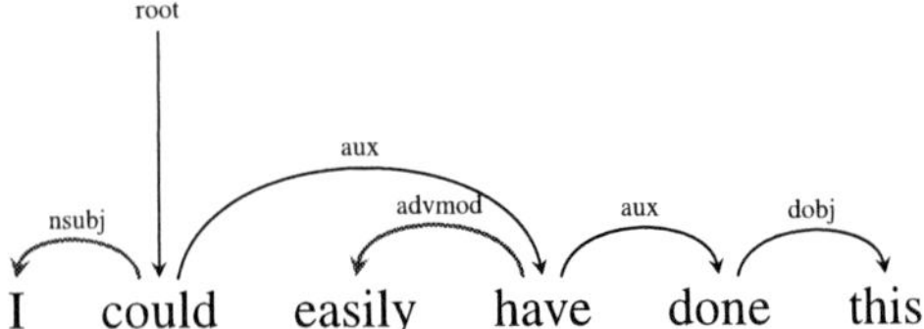

Figure 5: Example (1) annotated in MS style. Thick blue dependencies are those that changed compared to Figure 4.

w_{aux} is added to that V_i's set of auxiliaries $V_{i_{aux}}$. Otherwise, a new V_i is created and added to V.

After that, for each V_i in V, if there is only one auxiliary in $V_{i_{aux}}$, the direction of the dependency relation between that auxiliary and the main verb $V_{i_{mv}}$ is inverted and the head of $V_{i_{mv}}$ becomes the head of the auxiliary. When there are several auxiliaries (like in example (1)), the algorithm attaches the closest one to $V_{i_{mv}}$ and the head of $V_{i_{mv}}$ becomes the head of the outermost one. Any auxiliary in-between is attached in a chain from the outermost to the one that is closest to the verb. In the example, the main verb *done* gets attached to the closest auxiliary *have* and the head of the main verb *done* which was the root becomes the head of the outermost auxiliary, *could*.

Next, dependents of the main verb are dealt with to make sure projectivity is maintained. As a matter of fact, as can be seen from Figure 4, the previous changes can introduce non-projectivity in an otherwise projective tree, which is undesirable. Dependents to the left of the leftmost verb of the whole verb group (i.e. including the auxiliaries and the main verb) get attached to the leftmost verb. In the example, *I* gets attached to *could*. Dependents to the right of the rightmost verb of the verb group get attached to the leftmost verb. In the example, *this* remains attached to the main verb *done*. Any remaining dependent gets attached to the auxiliary that is closest to the verb. In the example, *easily* gets attached to *have*.

3.3 Back Transformation Algorithm

The back transformation algorithm works similarly to the transformation algorithm. A set of verb groups V is first collected by traversing the sentence from left to right, looking at auxiliary dependency relations. An auxiliary dependency relation $w_d \xleftarrow{aux} w_h$ between a dependent w_d and a head w_h

in MS can be between an auxiliary and the main verb or between two auxiliaries. When one such relation is found, if its head w_h is not already in a $V_{i_{aux}}$ in V, a new verb group V_i is created and w_h is added to $V_{i_{aux}}$. What the algorithm does next depends on the direction of that dependency relation. If it is right-headed, the dependent w_d of that dependency relation is the main verb and the algorithm recurses the chain of auxiliary dependency relations through heads: it looks at the head w_h of dependency relations and adds them to $V_{i_{aux}}$ until it finds a head that is not itself the dependent of an auxiliary dependency relation. If it is left-headed, the algorithm recurses the chain of auxiliary dependency relations through the dependents. It looks at dependents of dependency relations until it finds the main verb $V_{i_{mv}}$, i.e. a w_{i_d} that is not the head of an auxiliary dependency relation, each time adding the head of the relation w_{i_h} to $V_{i_{aux}}$. After that, for each V_i in V, the head of the auxiliary that is furthest from the main verb becomes the head of the main verb. The main verb becomes the head of all auxiliaries and their dependents.

In the previous example, Figure 5 can be transformed back to Figure 3 in this way: *done* is identified as the main verb of the verb group and *could* as its furthest auxiliary. The head of *could* therefore becomes the head of *done* and the two auxiliaries of the sentence as well as their dependents get attached to the main verb.

3.4 Data

We ran all experiments on UD 1.2 (Nivre et al., 2015). Treebanks that had 0.1% or less of auxiliary dependency relations were discarded. Japanese was also discarded because the Japanese treebank is not open source. Dutch was discarded because the back transformation accuracy was low (90%). This is due to inconsistencies in the annotation: verb groups are annotated as a chain of dependency relations. This leaves us with a total of 25 out of the 37 treebanks. For comparability with the study in Nilsson et al. (2007), and because we used a slightly modified version of their algorithm, we also tested the approach on the versions of the Czech and Slovenian treebanks that they worked on, respectively version 1.0 of the PDT (Hajic et al., 2001) and the 2006 version of SDT (Deroski et al., 2006). Table 1 gives an

Treebank	#S	#W	%A
SDT	1,936	35K	9.45
PDT	80,407	1,382K	1.38
Basque	7,194	97K	8.51
Bulgarian	10,022	141K	1.03
Croatian	3,757	84K	3.87
Czech	77,765	1,333K	0.92
Danish	5,190	95K	2.29
English	14,545	230K	2.85
Estonian	1,184	9K	0.73
Finnish	12,933	172K	1.49
Finnish-FTB	16,913	143K	2.89
French	16,148	394K	1.45
German	14,917	282K	1.05
Greek	2,170	53K	0.36
Hebrew	5,725	147K	0.15
Hindi	14,963	316K	3.27
Italian	12,188	260K	1.87
Norwegian	18,106	281K	2.60
Old_Church_Slavonic	5,782	52K	0.35
Persian	5,397	137K	1.40
Polish	7,500	76K	0.97
Portuguese	9,071	207K	0.20
Romanian	557	11K	2.88
Slovenian	7,206	126K	4.57
Spanish	15,739	424K	0.89
Swedish	4,807	76K	2.37
Tamil	480	8K	5.30

Table 1: Data sets: train + development; S= sentence, W=word; A=auxiliary dependency relation.

overview of the data used for the experiments.

3.5 Software

For comparability with previous studies, we used MaltParser (Nivre et al., 2006) with default settings, training on the training set and parsing on the development set for all the languages that we investigated. For enhanced comparability of the results, we used the UD POS tags instead of the language specific POS tags. MaltEval (Nilsson and Nivre, 2008) was used for evaluation. The transformation code has been released as part of the python package oDETTE version 1.0[2] (DEpendency Treebank Transformation and Evaluation). The package can be used to run the whole pipeline, from transformation to evaluation. It can work on several treebanks in parallel which enables quick experiments. (We trained and parsed the data for the 25 treebanks in 9 minutes on an 8-core machine).

[2]https://github.com/mdelhoneux/oDETTE/archive/v1.0.tar.gz

4   Results

4.1   Effect of VG Transformation on Parsing

As mentioned before, we converted training data in all treebanks involved, trained a parser with that transformed training set, parsed the test data and transformed the parsed data back to the original representation. Parsing accuracy of that transformed parsed data can then be compared with the parsed data obtained from the baseline, the unmodified model. Results are given in Table 2. All results report Labeled Attachment Scores (henceforth LAS) using MaltParser. As Unlabeled Attachment Scores (UAS) showed similar tendencies to LAS, they are not included for clarity. All experiments report significance levels for the McNemar test as obtained by MaltEval.[3]   A 100% accuracy was obtained for the back transformation of all data sets except for UD Spanish, Portuguese, Romanian and Hindi (99.9, 99.7, 99.4 and 99% respectively). As can be seen from the table and contrary to expectations, by and large the results decrease significantly with the transformed version of the treebank with a few exceptions but no result increases significantly.

As mentioned in Section 2.1, results on the original representation are the ones that we care about because it is the UD representation that we are interested in and because those results are directly comparable with each other. However, as was also said, results on the transformed gold standard can give an indication on the learnability of a construction. For this reason, they are reported in Table 3. Table 3 also reports results of the parsing model trained on UD representations where the parsed data have been transformed to the MS representation. As was said in Section 3.1, this is to find out if error amplifications have a strong influence on the results: if error amplifications were the main source of added errors from the baseline on UD to the back transformed UD, it would be expected that the original parsed test set transformed into MS would perform worse on the MS gold standard than the test set parsed by the model trained on MS. As can be seen from Table 3 however, this is not the case: the original model generally beats the transformed model even on the transformed gold standard. As can also be seen from the

[3]In the tables, $* = p < .05$ and $** = p < .01$.

UD language	Orig	Transf
Basque	**64.4**	63.8**
Bulgarian	**83.4**	83.2*
Croatian	**75.9**	74.6**
Czech	**80.0**	76.5**
Danish	**75.9**	75.2**
English	**81.7**	80.4**
Estonian	77.1	**77.8**
Finnish	**66.9**	66.4*
Finnish-FTB	**71.3**	70.4**
French	**82.1**	81.6**
German	**76.6**	76.0**
Greek	75.2	**75.3**
Hebrew	**78.4**	77.9**
Hindi	**85.4**	84.2**
Italian	**83.8**	83.6
Norwegian	**84.5**	82.0**
Old_Church_Slavonic	**68.8**	68.7
Persian	**81.1**	79.8**
Polish	**79.4**	79.1
Portuguese	81.3	**81.5**
Romanian	**64.2**	62.5*
Slovenian	**80.8**	79.7**
Spanish	**81.5**	81.2**
Swedish	**76.8**	75.7**
Tamil	**67.2**	67.1

Table 2: LAS with the original and transformed treebanks.

UD language/ Gold	Orig UD	Orig MS	Transf MS
Basque	**64.4**	**64.4**	64.0
Bulgarian	**83.4**	82.9	*82.5*
Croatian	**75.9**	**75.9**	73.7
Czech	**80.0**	*79.9*	76.4
Danish	**75.9**	*75.8*	74.8
English	**81.7**	*81.5*	80.2
Estonian	*77.1*	77.0	**77.6**
Finnish	**66.9**	66.4	65.9
Finnish-FTB	71.3	**72.5**	*72.1*
French	**82.1**	*81.8*	81.3
German	**76.6**	*76.1*	75.4
Greek	**75.2**	**75.2**	75.1
Hebrew	*78.4*	**78.5**	77.9
Hindi	**85.4**	*85.2*	84.9
Italian	**83.8**	*83.6*	83.3
Norwegian	**84.5**	**84.5**	81.7
Old_Church_Slavonic	*68.8*	**68.9**	68.7
Persian	**81.1**	**81.1**	79.8
Polish	**79.4**	*79.3*	79.0
Portuguese	**81.3**	**81.3**	81.6
Romanian	*64.2*	**64.6**	64.0
Slovenian	**80.8**	**80.8**	79.8
Spanish	**81.5**	*81.4*	81.2
Swedish	**76.8**	*76.7*	75.6
Tamil	67.2	**67.5**	*67.4*

Table 3: LAS on original and transformed treebanks on original gold standard (UD) and transformed (MS). Highest score in bold and second highest in Italics.

table, the scores are overall higher for the UD parsing model on the UD gold standard than the transformed parsing model on the transformed gold standard. This potentially indicates that the verb group transformation makes the UD representation harder to learn and might help give a partial explanation of why it decreases parsing accuracy on the original gold standard. This is not entirely surprising as, as can be seen from the Figures illustrating the transformation above, the original representation is flatter than the transformed representation. Further work is needed to explore that more in-depth. In any case, the original model beats the transformed model on several metrics and it seems safe to conclude that the verb group transformation hurts UD parsing at least with MaltParser.

4.2 Comparing Dependency Relations

Turning to the error analysis, one thing that is striking when looking at the performance of different dependency relations is that punctuation performs consistently worse in the transformed version of the parsed data compared to the baseline as can be seen in Figure 6.[4]

Because punctuation is most often attached to the main verb, it can be hypothesized that identifying the main verb of the sentence is crucial for avoiding this kind of errors and that the transformation hurts the identification of the main verb in the case of UD. A close examination of about a third of errors containing an auxiliary dependency relation in English further reinforced that hypothesis.

4.3 Comparison with SDT and PDT

What is noticeable in the results we have seen so far is that the accuracy decreased for languages for which accuracy has been shown to increase in the past: Czech, Slovenian and English. This indicates that the UD style is making a difference. For that reason, we are now attempting a comparison be-

---

[4]Punctuation is often excluded from evaluation for several reasons so it is important to say that although punctuation is affected by the score, the overall trend in the evaluation does not change if it is excluded which indicates that its decrease in accuracy is a symptom of what is going on.

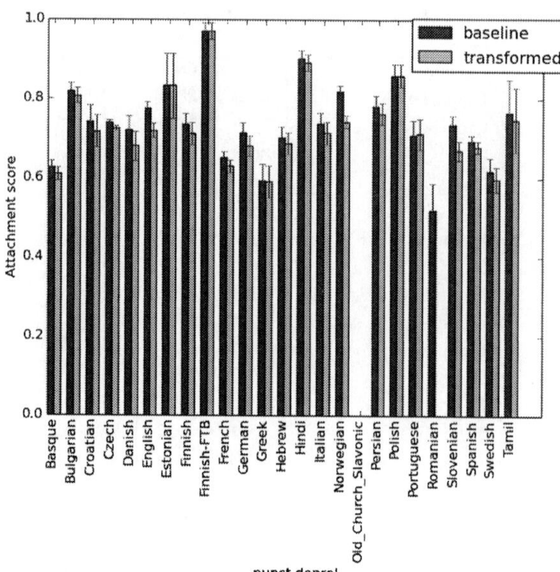

Figure 6: F1 score and error margin in parsed test set

	Orig	Transf
UD_Czech	**80.0**	76.5**
PDT	68.5	**68.8**
UD_Slovenian	**80.5**	79.1**
SDT	65.7	**66.2**

Table 4: LAS with the original and transformed treebanks.

	Orig	Transf	Δ
SDT τ_d	**67.8**	67.4	-0.4
SDT τ_o	65.7	**66.2**	0.5
SDT τ_a	64.2	**65.4***	1.2
PDT τ_d	69.2	69.2	0.0
PDT τ_o	68.5	**68.8**	0.3
PDT τ_a	68.2	**68.4***	0.2

Table 5: LAS on the original and transformed treebanks with different levels of POS tag ambiguity. Δ = Transf - Orig

tween the effect of the approach on SDT and on UD_Slovenian as well as between its effect on PDT and UD_Czech. As shown in Table 4, similar improvements to the original study were obtained on SDT and PDT.

As was just mentioned, it can be hypothesized that identifying the main verb is crucial for avoiding the kind of errors that were observed in the UD transformed version. It can then be hypothesized that the transformation helps to identify the main verb in PDT and SDT whereas it makes it harder in UD. When observing some examples in SDT, the transformation seems to help disambiguating POS tags. As a matter of fact, more than 90% of auxiliaries in SDT have the tag *Verb-copula* but also more than 20% of the main verbs involved in auxiliary dependency relations have that same POS tag. POS tags therefore do not give enough information to distinguish between the main verb and an auxiliary.

The experiment we are now turning to suggested that this is a reasonable hypothesis. We tested the approach on three different versions of PDT and

SDT (i.e. we changed both training and test data, trained the model on the transformed training set, parsed on transformed test set and compared with the transformed gold standard). In the original version τ_o, we did not change anything. We created a disambiguated version τ_d, in which main verbs are tagged as *Verb-main* for SDT, and *Vp* for PDT and where auxiliaries are tagged *aux*. We created an ambiguous version τ_a, where we made verbs fully ambiguous, i.e. all verbal tags are transformed to the same *verb* POS tag.

As appears from Table 5, the results in SDT support the hypothesis: when verbs are made fully ambiguous, the transformation improves the results more than when they are partially ambiguous. When they are disambiguated, the approach does not work, the accuracy even decreases. The picture is slightly less clear with PDT where disambiguating the POS tags makes the approach ineffective but making them ambiguous does not make the approach more useful. Ambiguating the tags seems to affect PDT less than it affects SDT however which might indicate that PDT suffers from ambiguity even more than SDT in the original treebank. This might be due to the fact that the POS tags used in the PDT experiments are automatically predicted whereas the tags used for SDT are gold tags. This idea is further explored in Section 4.4.

We tested the same approach on the UD treebanks for Czech and Slovenian to see if they can also be affected by ambiguity in some way. In the case of UD, τ_d is the same as τ_o since the tags are already disambiguated. As can be seen from the top part of Table 6, the opposite effect is found: the transformation hurts accuracy more when the tags are ambiguous than when they are not. However, because of the similarity between copulas and auxiliaries in UD, representing them differently might make it confus-

	Orig	Transf	Δ
UD_Slovenian τ_o	80.8	79.7**	-1.1
UD_Slovenian τ_a	79.7	77.1**	-2.6
UD_Czech τ_o	77.1	76.6**	-0.5
UD_Czech τ_a	76.7	76.1**	-0.6
Without copula dependency relations			
UD_Slovenian τ_o	85.4	83.6**	-1.8
UD_Slovenian τ_a	83.6	82.2**	-1.4
UD_Czech τ_o	79.1	78.7**	-0.4
UD_Czech τ_a	78.3	78.1**	-0.2

Table 6: LAS on the original and transformed treebanks with different levels of POS tag ambiguity. Δ = Transf - Orig

POS tag	Orig	Transf	Δ
gold	76.8	75.7**	-1.1
predicted	76.4	75.6**	-0.8

Table 7: LAS on the original and transformed UD_Swedish treebank with predicted and gold POS tags. Δ = Transf - Orig

ing for the parser. It would be interesting to try the approach and change the representation of copulas as well as auxiliaries. We tested something simpler: we tested the same experiment on the treebanks without copulas, i.e. we removed all sentences that have a copula dependency relations both in the training and the test sets. As can be seen from the bottom of Table 6, doing so gives the expected results: the transformation affects accuracy less when the tags are ambiguous than when they are not. The transformation still does not help parsing accuracy however.

4.4 Predicted vs gold POS tags

An issue that has been ignored so far is that in the PDT, the parser used predicted POS tags for parsing the test sets whereas in UD (and in SDT), we have been using gold POS tags. It was said in the previous section that the experiment about ambiguity on the PDT seems to indicate that tags are of poorer quality in the original experiment. It is possible that this is due to the fact that they are predicted rather than gold tags. It would be interesting to find out if the transformation approach works on UD parsing using predicted tags. This is slightly difficult to test as there does not exist taggers for all UD treebanks yet. There does exist one for Swedish however, which is why we tested this hypothesis on UD_Swedish. As can be seen from Table 7, using predicted POS tags does have an impact on the effect of the transformation as the transformation hurts parsing accuracy less than it does on data with gold POS tags. The transformation still does not help parsing accuracy however.

Overall then, the results suggest that there is something about the UD representation that makes this transformation infelicitous. It seems then that in the case of UD, it is better to keep the main verbs as heads of auxiliary dependency relations. There are other factors that may play a role in the results. For example, as appears from Table 1, the original SDT has a much higher percentage of auxiliary dependencies. This could be caused by the domain of the treebank.

5 Conclusion and Future Work

In this paper, we have attempted to reproduce a study by Nilsson et al. (2007) that has shown that making auxiliaries heads in verb groups improves parsing but failed to show that those results port to parsing with Universal Dependencies. Contrary to expectations, the study has given evidence that main verbs should stay heads of auxiliary dependency relations for parsing with UD. The benefits of error analyses for such a study have been highlighted because they allow us to shed more light on the different ways in which the transformations affect the parsing output. Experiments suggest that gains obtained from verb group transformations in previous studies have been obtained mainly because those transformations help disambiguating between main verbs and auxiliaries. It is however still an open question why the VG transformation hurts parsing accuracy in the case of UD. It seems that the transformation makes the construction harder to learn which might be because it makes it less flat. Future work could carry out an error analysis that is more detailed than was the case in this study. Repeating those experiments with other tree transformations that have been shown to be successful in the past, such as making prepositions the head of prepositional phrases, as well as looking at other parsing models would provide more insight into the relationship between tree transformations and parsing.

Acknowledgements

We thank the three anonymous reviewers for useful feedback. We would also like to thank Jimmy Callin and Huener Kasikara for useful comments on a first version of this paper. Discussions with the participants of the course Language Technology: Research and Development in Uppsala also provided valuable help for this project. Thanks to Aaron Smith for providing the predicted POS tags data set for UD_Swedish.

References

Michael Collins. 1999. *Head-driven Statistical Models for Natural Language Parsing*. Ph.D. thesis, University of Pennsylvania.

Marie-Catherine de Marneffe, Timothy Dozat, Natalia Silveira, Katri Haverinen, Filip Ginter, Joakim Nivre, and Christopher D. Manning. 2014. Universal stanford dependencies: A cross-linguistic typology. In *Proceedings of the Ninth International Conference on Language Resources and Evaluation (LREC-2014), Reykjavik, Iceland, May 26-31, 2014.*. pages 4585–4592.

Sao Deroski, Toma Erjavec, Nina Ledinek, Petr Pajas, Zdenk abokrtsk, and Andreja ele. 2006. Towards a slovene dependency treebank. In *Proceedings of the 5th International Conference on Language Resources and Evaluation (LREC 2006)*. ELRA, Genova, Italy, pages 1388–1391.

Jan Hajic, Eva Hajicova, Petr Pajas, Jarmila Panevova, and Petr Sgall. 2001. Prague dependency treebank 1.0. LDC, 2001T10.

Ryan McDonald and Joakim Nivre. 2007. Characterizing the errors of data-driven dependency parsing models. In *Proceedings of the 2007 Joint Conference on Empirical Methods in Natural Language Processing and Computational Natural Language Learning (EMNLP-CoNLL)*. pages 122–131.

I.A. Melčuk. 1988. *Dependency Syntax: Theory and Practice*. SUNY series in Linguistics. State University of New York Press.

Jens Nilsson and Joakim Nivre. 2008. MaltEval: An evaluation and visualization tool for dependency parsing. In *Proceedings of the Sixth International Conference on Language Resources and Evaluation (LREC)*. pages 161–166.

Jens Nilsson, Joakim Nivre, and Johan Hall. 2006. Graph transformations in data-driven dependency parsing. In *Proceedings of the 21st International Conference on Computational Linguistics and the 44th Annual Meeting of the Association for Computational Linguistics*. Association for Computational Linguistics, Stroudsburg, PA, USA, ACL-44, pages 257–264.

Jens Nilsson, Joakim Nivre, and Johan Hall. 2007. Generalizing tree transformations for inductive dependency parsing. In *ACL 2007, Proceedings of the 45th Annual Meeting of the Association for Computational Linguistics, June 23-30, 2007, Prague, Czech Republic*.

Joakim Nivre. 2015. Towards a universal grammar for natural language processing. In *Computational Linguistics and Intelligent Text Processing - 16th International Conference, CICLing 2015, Cairo, Egypt, April 14-20, 2015, Proceedings, Part I*. pages 3–16.

Joakim Nivre, Željko Agić, Maria Jesus Aranzabe, Masayuki Asahara, Aitziber Atutxa, Miguel Ballesteros, John Bauer, Kepa Bengoetxea, Riyaz Ahmad Bhat, Cristina Bosco, Sam Bowman, Giuseppe G. A. Celano, Miriam Connor, Marie-Catherine de Marneffe, Arantza Diaz de Ilarraza, Kaja Dobrovoljc, Timothy Dozat, Tomaž Erjavec, Richárd Farkas, Jennifer Foster, Daniel Galbraith, Filip Ginter, Iakes Goenaga, Koldo Gojenola, Yoav Goldberg, Berta Gonzales, Bruno Guillaume, Jan Hajič, Dag Haug, Radu Ion, Elena Irimia, Anders Johannsen, Hiroshi Kanayama, Jenna Kanerva, Simon Krek, Veronika Laippala, Alessandro Lenci, Nikola Ljubešić, Teresa Lynn, Christopher Manning, Ctlina Mrnduc, David Mareček, Héctor Martínez Alonso, Jan Mašek, Yuji Matsumoto, Ryan McDonald, Anna Missilä, Verginica Mititelu, Yusuke Miyao, Simonetta Montemagni, Shunsuke Mori, Hanna Nurmi, Petya Osenova, Lilja Øvrelid, Elena Pascual, Marco Passarotti, Cenel-Augusto Perez, Slav Petrov, Jussi Piitulainen, Barbara Plank, Martin Popel, Prokopis Prokopidis, Sampo Pyysalo, Loganathan Ramasamy, Rudolf Rosa, Shadi Saleh, Sebastian Schuster, Wolfgang Seeker, Mojgan Seraji, Natalia Silveira, Maria Simi, Radu Simionescu, Katalin Simkó, Kiril Simov, Aaron Smith, Jan Štěpánek, Alane Suhr, Zsolt Szántó, Takaaki Tanaka, Reut Tsarfaty, Sumire Uematsu,

Larraitz Uria, Viktor Varga, Veronika Vincze, Zdeněk Žabokrtský, Daniel Zeman, and Hanzhi Zhu. 2015. Universal dependencies 1.2. LIN-DAT/CLARIN digital library at Institute of Formal and Applied Linguistics, Charles University in Prague.

Joakim Nivre, Johan Hall, and Jens Nilsson. 2006. MaltParser: A data-driven parser-generator for dependency parsing. In *Proceedings of the 5th International Conference on Language Resources and Evaluation (LREC)*. pages 2216–2219.

Roy Schwartz, Omri Abend, and Ari Rappoport. 2012. Learnability-based syntactic annotation design. In *COLING*. volume 24, pages 2405–2422.

Natalia Silveira and Christopher Manning. 2015. Does Universal Dependencies need a parsing representation? An investigation of English. In *Proceedings of the Third International Conference on Dependency Linguistics (Depling 2015)*. pages 310–319.

Cross-lingual Dependency Transfer : What Matters?
Assessing the Impact of Pre- and Post-processing

Ophélie Lacroix, Guillaume Wisniewski and **François Yvon**
LIMSI, CNRS, Univ. Paris-Sud, Université Paris-Saclay, F-91405 Orsay
{ophelie.lacroix, guillaume.wisniewski, francois.yvon}@limsi.fr

Abstract

In this paper, we propose to analyze the pre- and post-processing steps applied in the context of cross-lingual dependency transfer. To this aim, we employ a simple transfer strategy that operates on partially annotated projected data. We show that a good data selection strategy is a key point in successfully transferring dependencies and that better data selection techniques need to be developed in order to achieve the performance of fully supervised methods.

1 Introduction

Supervised learning techniques nowadays lie at the core of most Natural Language Processing (NLP) tools. Their use is however hindered by the scarcity of annotated data, which are only available for a restricted number of tasks, genres, domain, and languages. The supervision information that exists for well-resourced languages can however be transferred to under-resourced languages through the use of cross-lingual techniques. In this work, we focus on the transfer of syntactic dependency annotations.

Two main transfer strategies have been proposed in the literature: direct transfer model and annotation transfer. The first approach is mainly based on delexicalized parsing (Zeman and Resnik, 2008; McDonald et al., 2011) which assumes of common morpho-syntactic representation (e.g. PoS tags) between the source and target languages. It has been improved with the use of self-training, data selection, relexicalization and multi-source transfer (Naseem et al., 2010; Cohen et al., 2011; Søgaard, 2011; Täckström et al., 2013).

The second approach (transfer of annotations), relies on parallel corpora to project, through alignment links, the dependencies automatically predicted from a resource-rich language to a resource-poor language. This approach pioneered by Hwa et al. (2005) requires various heuristic transformation rules to cope with the non-isomorphism between the source and target structures as well as with the noise in source annotations and in alignments. It has since enjoyed a great popularity and been improved by many works (see the overview in Section 2).

In spite of the simplicity of the annotation transfer principle, all these methods have several (hidden) parameters, such as the symmetrization heuristic or filtering thresholds, that make any direct comparison of their performance very hard. That is why, in this work, we aim at analyzing the impact of external factors used as pre- and post-processing steps and their significance in the whole transfer process. To this end, we propose to use the simple transfer strategy exploiting partially annotated data introduced in Lacroix et al. (2016) to systematically compare various design decisions.

The transfer strategy used in our experiments is explained in Section 2. We then propose to explore and analyze different external factors: projected data filtering (Section 3.1), enhancement of the parsing strategy (Section 3.2) and multi-source transfer (Section 3.3). Finally, we compare the efficiency of dependency transfer and supervised parsing (Section 3.4) and analyze the performance achieved for the different kind of labels (Section 3.5).

Proceedings of the Workshop on Multilingual and Cross-lingual Methods in NLP, pages 20–29,
San Diego, California, June 17, 2016. ©2016 Association for Computational Linguistics

2   Transfer strategy

In this Section, we describe the two main steps of the transfer process considered in our experiments: the projection of the dependencies through word alignments from a source language to a target language and the training method of Lacroix et al. (2016) for transition-based parser that can learn a parser from partial dependency trees. We also present the dataset used in our experiments and evaluate the proposed approach.

2.1   Dependency Projection

Most works on dependency transfer use a similar setting. They consider sentence-aligned bitexts for which an automatically parsed text in a resource-rich language is associated with its translation in a target language. Parallel sentences are then aligned in both directions and these alignments are merged with a symmetrization heuristics. To further guarantee their quality, alignments are generally filtered using various hand-crafted rules, for instance, to remove alignment links that associate words with different PoS tags (Rasooli and Collins, 2015) or sentences in which the number of alignment links is too low. Finally dependencies are projected through alignment links.

Dependencies for which both the head and the dependent are each aligned to exactly one word (i.e. $1:1$ alignment) can be readily transferred to the target language. Difficulties with the projection arise with many-to-many links and un-aligned tokens. Some heuristics were proposed by Hwa et al. (2005), and reused by Tiedemann (2014), to deal with these multiple alignments. Nonetheless, to avoid this problem several works have proposed ad hoc rules to complete the trees. For instance, Spreyer and Kuhn (2009) propose to attach unaligned tokens to a fake root in order to ignore the actions associated with these dependencies during learning; Li et al. (2014) choose to add all dependency possibilities of the unaligned tokens to preserve ambiguity during learning; Ma and Xia (2014) consider, the potentially noisy, dependencies predicted by a delexicalized parser. Applying these heuristics allows, at the expense of adding potentially fake tokens or noisy dependencies, to label automatically a corpus of full parsing trees in the target language on which a stan-

dard learning method can be used.

In this work, we consider another approach and choose to ignore unattached words as well as many-to-many alignments: we focus on the projection through $1:1$ alignments that are, intuitively, the most reliable. More precisely, to prevent annotations of noisy dependencies to be transferred, we decide to remove all multiple alignment links, and among the remaining links, we remove the ones that associate words with different PoS (following the soft rules proposed by Rasooli and Collins (2015)). After projection, we filter the sentences in which less than 80% of the words receive a dependency as they often result from bad quality alignments. At the end, we obtain an automatically annotated corpus for the target language that contains partial but accurate annotations.[1] We will describe, in the following Section, how a parser can be trained on such data.

In spite of its simplicity, this way to transfer dependency has several (hidden) parameters, such as the symmetrization heuristic or the filtering threshold, that can have a large impact on the quality of the transferred parser. We will evaluate, in Section 3 trough 3.1 the impact of these design decisions.

2.2   Partial Transition-based Learning

We consider a transition-based dependency parser based on the arc-eager algorithm (Nivre, 2003): this parser builds a dependency tree incrementally by performing a sequence of *actions*. At each step of the parsing process, a classifier scores each possible action and the highest scoring one is applied.

Training relies on the dynamic oracle of Goldberg and Nivre (2012): for each sentence, a parse tree is built incrementally; at each step, if the predicted action creates an erroneous dependency (or, equivalently, prevents the creation of a gold dependency), a weight vector is updated, according to the perceptron rule. The set of all 'correct' actions is built considering the (potentially wrong) predicted tree and the gold action is defined as the correct action with the highest model score.

It is crucial to note that the training algorithm is an

---

[1] We also remove from target sentences containing non-projective dependencies, as sentences containing non-projective dependencies often results in low-quality projected dependency structures (Mareček, 2011) and cannot be taken into account in the standard ARCEAGER training method.

error-correction learning procedure that solely relies on its capacity to detect when an action choice will result in an error: when no error is detected, the construction of the parse tree continues according to the model prediction. Consequently, this training procedure can also be used, as such, to train a dependency parser from partially annotated data: when no supervision information is available (no correct dependencies are known), all actions are considered as correct; in this case, the predicted action is necessarily equal to the correct action, the weight vector is not updated, and the training process goes on.

2.3 Dataset

All our experiments are carried out on six languages[2] of the Universal Dependency Treebank Project v2.0 (UDT) (McDonald et al., 2013): German (de), English (en), Spanish (es), French (fr), Italian (it) and Swedish (sv). We consider as parallel corpora a subset of the Europarl corpus that have exactly the same English sentences, collecting $1,231,216$ parallel sentences for the 6 language pairs.

For the evaluation, the original splits (train/test/dev) of the UDT corpora are kept for training the source and evaluate the target.

2.4 Experiments

The parallel sentences are aligned in both directions with `Giza++` (Och and Ney, 2003). These alignments are then merged with the intersection and grow-diag heuristics. For each language pair, the source dataset (Europarl) is PoS-tagged and parsed using the transition-based version of the MateParser (Bohnet and Nivre, 2012) with a beam of 40, which was trained on the UDT corpus. These predicted annotations are then partially projected on the target language data using the projection strategy described in Section 2.1.

To train a parser on partially projected target data, we used our own implementation of the arc-eager dependency parser, using the features described in Zhang and Nivre (2011). The greedy version of the parser is used in all but one experiments of the Section 3 while a beam-search (with a beam-size of 8 for learning & parsing) is used to achieve

---

²These are the languages present in both Europarl and UDT.

the best performances of the proposed method (Section 2.5).[3]

2.5 Performance

We present the results of our transfer strategy in the table 1. The results are first presented for cross-lingual transfer from English and second, applying a voting method for transferring from multiple source languages.[4] These scores are obtained using the most appropriate external factors: filtering of the projected sentences for which less than 80% words are attached, beam-search strategy for parsing the source and target data. The effects of this parameters on the transfer results are clarified respectively in sections 3.1 and 3.2.

This method achieves results that are competitive with recent state-of-the-art methods such as (Ma and Xia, 2014; Rasooli and Collins, 2015), at a much cheaper computational cost,[5] which allows us to make all the experiments required to compare the various design decisions. The results of Table 1 also show that using the grow-diag heuristic to symmetrize the alignments rather than the intersection heuristic hurts performance for all languages.

		intersection		grow-diag		sup.
source		(en)	(multi)	(en)	(multi)	
target	de	73.7	76.8	71.2	75.6	84.4
	es	76.8	79.3	75.4	79.0	85.5
	fr	77.9	80.9	76.7	81.0	85.8
	it	77.8	80.1	76.2	80.1	86.9
	sv	82.1	83.3	80.1	83.1	87.8

Table 1: Results of our transfer method. 'sup' present the fully supervised scores.

3 Analysis

3.1 The importance of filtering

To assess the usefulness of filtering on transfer performance, we conduct experiments on several lan-

---

³The beam search parser used in our experiments is described in (Aufrant and Wisniewski, 2016)

⁴For a target language, projection is applied from each of the other 5 languages. For each token of a sentence the most frequent head among the projected heads is saved (from the most frequent one to the less) if it does not impede the projectivity of the resulted tree (which then can be partially annotated).

⁵See (Lacroix et al., 2016) for more details.

guage pairs, considering two symmetrization heuristics: the intersection and the grow-diag heuristics. After the projection step, several greedy parsers are learned for increasing sizes of projected datasets. The sentences are included in the learning set in order of decreasing percentage of attached tokens.

The results for French, German and Swedish are presented respectively in Figure 1. Similar curves are obtained for Italian and Spanish. These results show that adding partially annotated sentences improves parsing performance as long as these sentences have enough attached tokens. For instance, in French (focusing on the scores obtained with the intersection heuristics), a parser trained only on fully labelled sentences achieves a UAS of 75.6%; when sentences in which more than 80% of dependencies are known are added, parsing performance is improved to 76.9%, but adding more sentences hurts performance. Indeed, sentences with a small number of attached tokens correspond to sentence pairs with few alignment links that are often not perfect translation of each other and may have very different grammatical structures.

One can notice that, while the number of sentences needed to reach the top scores varies greatly from a language to another, the average percentage of attached token per sentence remains in a short interval (from 74.9 % (de) to 84.9 % (sv)). Adding more sparse data seems to bring more noise than relevant syntactic information. Controlling the quality of the projected data, over the quantity, is therefore a key point in the success of the transfer process. This observation justifies our decision to consider only sentences with more than 80% of attached tokens.

Finally, the scores obtained with the use of the heuristic of symetrization intersection are mostly higher than those obtained with the grow-diag heuristic. It is worth noting that the number of sentences fully annotated with the grow-diag heuristic is far less important than with the intersection. For instance in French, the training filtered data contains 21,381 sentences when the intersection heuristic is used, but only 6,534 for the grow-diag heuristic. Indeed, the number of projected dependencies is lower because multiple alignments impede the projection of dependencies. This restrains the projection of potentially wrong dependencies from ambiguous alignments but also the diversity of the syn-

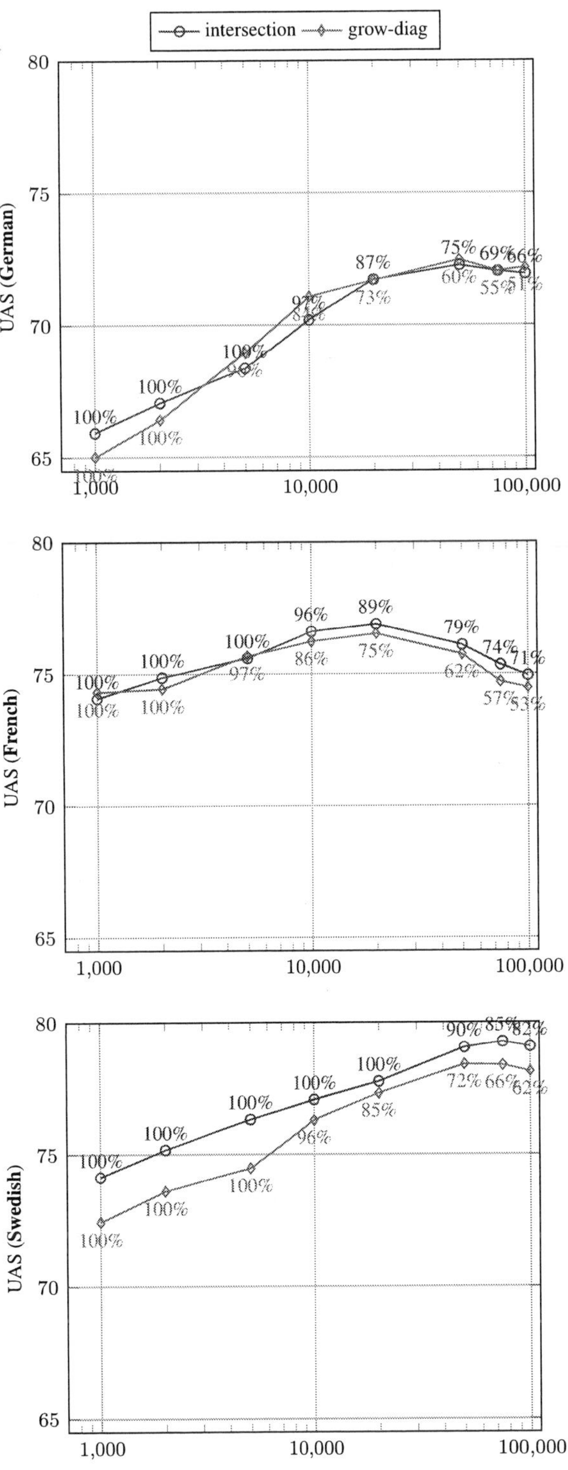

Figure 1: Variation of the transfer scores (UAS) depending on the number of sentences selected for learning. For each node the average percentage of attached token per sentence is specified. Greedy target parsing. Evaluation on gold PoS-tagged data.

tactic information transferred on the target language, and then the parsing performances. In the rest of the paper we will only consider the intersection heuristic.

This experiment shows that an appropriate selection of the alignment strategy and thus of the projected data used for learning could benefit the transfer scores of the methods that exploit (raw or even completed) partial data.

3.2 Pumping the parsing

It is well known that different techniques can boost parsing performance. For instance, clusters (Koo et al., 2008) may be used to reduce lexical sparseness, which is particularly appropriate in the case of dependency parser transfer since parallel data are generally not from the same domain as the corpus used to train and evaluate the parser. Another approach for boosting parsing performance is the use of a beam-search strategy that reduces the number of search errors (Zhang and Nivre, 2012). In this section, we aim at assessing, first, how parsing performance of the source language impacts the quality of the transferred parser, and second, how using more 'advanced' parsing techniques may boost parsing in the target language.

Using a similar transfer process as in the previous section, we conduct experiments in which the source and target parsers will be progressively enriched: we consider, in a first experiment, a greedy parser to predict the dependencies of the source and target sentences; the source greedy parsers are then replaced by a beam-search parser and features describing Brown clusters learned from the Europarl data are added. Finally, we also consider a beam-search parser for parsing the target language, using our own implementation of the transition based parser presented in Section 2.2 with a beam size of 8, and enrich it with Brown clusters.

The transfer scores are presented in Table 2. First, these results show that the alignments are not good enough to reflect improvements in (source) parsing quality on the target data: the use of beam-search on parsing the source language allows an average improvement of 0.2 UAS point on the target languages, while the source (English) performance is improved by 2.3. The use of clusters does not improve the

Parsing strategy				Transfer target				
src		tgt		de	es	fr	it	sv
beam	clusters	beam	clusters					
-	-	-	-	71.3	75.6	76.3	76.2	79.9
✓	-	-	-	71.3	75.8	76.8	76.0	80.4
✓	✓	-	-	71.4	75.8	76.0	76.2	80.3
✓	✓	✓	-	73.5	**76.7**	**77.7**	**78.3**	**82.2**
✓	✓	✓	✓	**73.8**	76.7	**77.7**	78.0	81.9

Table 2: Transfer results according to the parsing strategy used on the source and target data. Evaluation, in UAS, on Gold PoS-tagged data.

average score, nor the source parsing performance.[6] However, the beam-search strategy is surely useful for parsing the projected target languages: scores are, on average, 1.34 higher. The use of clusters is not interesting: only German performance is improved ($+0.3$) while Italian and Swedish are both negatively impacted (-0.3 for both).

We have observed that the use of clusters is mostly useless in any case and, globally, that boosting the source parsing performance have very little effect on transfer final scores. However, not surprisingly, the use of beam-search for parsing the target data is highly effective for boosting the transfer scores.

3.3 Multisource impact

We have seen in Section 3.1 that filtering the projected data is a key point to achieve good transfer scores, as adding too much data for learning reduces the parsing performance. However, for a similar percentage of attached token, the number of sentences kept for learning varies a lot depending on the target language. For instance, when transferring from English, the number of sentences having more than 80% dependencies reaches 52,554 for Swedish but only 15,191 for German; the parsing scores differ greatly as well: their UAS is, respectively, 81.9 and 73.8. Spanish, Italian and French achieve relatively

---

[6]The inefficiency of clusters on English may be due to the fact that clusters are learned from Europarl data which are out-of-domain for the UDT data.

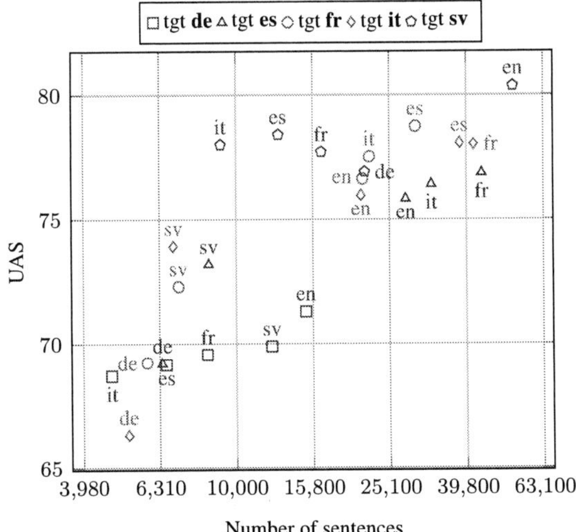

Figure 2: Results of the multi-lingual transfer depending on the number of sentences saved for learning. The label of each node indicates the source language and its color the target language.

close scores for the same order of number of sentences (around 20/30K).

These observations show that there is a correlation between the number of dependencies transferred and the parsing performance: the more filtered sentences there are the better the scores are. A natural way to increase the number of sentences with a high number of dependencies is to transfer dependencies from different languages: good projections result from good word alignments, that depend on source and target languages at stake.

We conduct multi-lingual experiments, similar to the experiments from English, in which each language (among German, Spanish, French, Italian and Swedish) is considered as the source language for the other ones. We consider as a parallel corpora a subset of the Europarl corpus (as detailed in Section 2.3). The sentences are filtered as previously after the dependencies have been transferred across alignment links. All reported results are achieved by a greedy parser considering gold PoS-tagged data.

The results of this multi-lingual experiment are presented in Figure 2, with, for every source language, the number of sentences that survived filtering.[7] These results show that, for each target language, the best score is achieved for the source language with the largest training set (which is: English for German and Swedish, French for Spanish and Italian, and Spanish for French). With the exception of Swedish, for a given target language, the UAS is proportional to the number of sentences, regardless of the source parsing performance.[8] As expected, languages from the same family, such as the ones derived from Latin (Spanish, French and Italian), are beneficial for each other. This observation has already been reported several times (e.g. by McDonald et al. (2013)), but Figure 2 suggests that the increase in performance may mainly result from a good alignment between the source and the target languages. Overall, these results stress the fact that the alignment quality has a large impact on the transfer performance and should not be neglected.

As seen in the previous section, the source parsing performance does not appear to be the parameter having the greatest impact on transfer. The quality of the alignment deriving from the choice of the source language is quite crucial.

3.4 Transfer vs Supervised Parsing

Cross-lingual transfer strategies are mainly used with the aim of developing swiftly NLP tools for resource-poor languages without the need of annotated corpora that are expensive to build from scratch. Results presented in the previous sections show that parsers trained on transferred data are still outperformed by supervised parsers. It is however difficult to evaluate how prejudicial this loss is. That is why, to assess the usefulness of transfer methods, we propose to determine the amount of gold annotated sentences needed to achieve performance similar to the performance of transferred parsers.

In a first series of experiments, we compare the performance of a cross-lingual dependency parser to supervised parsers learned from increasing amount of data (starting with 50 sentences). All the experiments are performed on 10 runs to mitigate the impact of selecting labelled data randomly, using the greedy version of the parser. Scores are evaluated on gold PoS-tagged data. The results, presented in Figure 3,[9] show that the amount of supervised

---

[7]It is important to note that the number of sentences is proportional to the number of dependencies.

[8]The source performances obtained with the MateParser (predicted PoS-tags) are: 92.4 (en), 80.4 (de), 83.1 (es), 83.8 (fr), 84.2 (it) and 85.7 (sv).

[9]Results for Spanish and Italian are quite similar to French.

data needed to achieve transfer scores are respectively around 250, 200 and 400 sentences for German, French and Swedish. This observation strongly question the interest of cross-lingual transfer: only a very limited amount of annotated data is required to outperform a parser trained on transferred annotations.

Wisniewski et al. (2014) show that the performance difference between a supervised and transferred PoS taggers partially results from divergences in annotation conventions and from evaluating the tagger on out-of-domain data: as in the setting described in Section 2, the taggers are trained on Europarl and evaluated on UDT. To assess the impact on parsing performance of this two elements, we propose, in a second series of experiments, to enrich the data labelled automatically by transferring annotations with an increasing amount of in-domain labelled data to learn new parsers.

Results of this experiments are presented in Figure 3. They show that a small amount of supervised data ($\simeq$ 300 sentences) provide useful information to projected data for parsing target languages: the performance of a parsers trained on the combination of transferred and labelled data outperforms both a parser trained on the labelled data only and a parser trained only on the transferred data. However above a specific threshold projected data become useless, and worse, adding them to labelled data hurts parsing performance. This could mean that the projected data, do not just lack syntactic diversity but also contain substantial amount of projection errors, even if the alignments have been filtered with very conservative rules.

3.5 Label scores and frequencies

The previous experiments suggest that cross-lingual parsers suffer from alignment errors (or from their absence) even if the alignments are filtered (restricted to $1:1$ and PoS-coherent links). To reveal systematic syntactic errors, we propose to examine the transfer scores depending on the (gold) syntactic label of the dependency. Our hypothesis is that the UAS of a given target label depends both on the capacity of the source parser to predict this label and on the ability of the transfer method to project the syntactic information. For the sake of clarity, we only report results for English to French transfer.

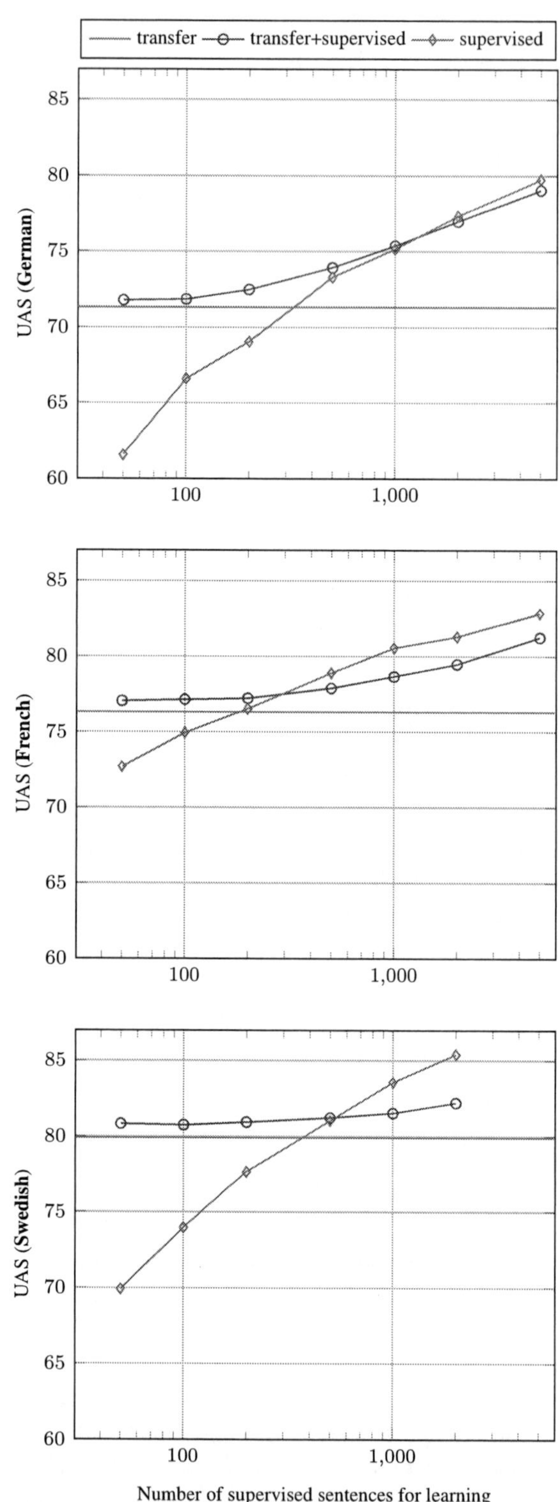

Figure 3: Evaluation of a parser for German learned from transferred and supervised data according to the number of included supervised data, and compared to fully supervised parsing. Greedy parsing. Evaluation on Gold PoS-tagged data.

Table 3 shows[10] the frequencies of the labels predicted by a supervised parser on the English and French EUROPARL corpora as well as the frequencies of these labels on the French projected (from English) and filtered data. It appears that the frequencies of the labels tend to look like the source frequencies, introducing a systematic bias in the data used to train a cross-lingual parser. In particular, some dependencies, such as the root, are over-projected but no label is entirely skipped. The syntactic information are quite proportionally transferred. Table 3 also reported the supervised UAS of these labels for English and French, as well as the UAS of the transferred parser for French. We observe that the prediction of each label suffers from transfer: each score is generally lower than the (source or target) supervised score. One can also notice that over-projection do not benefit label scores. Overall, it may suggest that projection errors are also quite proportionally transferred among the various labels.

Results of Table 3 also suggest that the capacity of the source parser to predict a given kind of dependency has not much impact on the performance of the target parser. For instance, the ADPOBJ and DET are both very well predicted by the English parser, but the prediction of the cross-lingual French parser are far better for DET than for ADPOBJ

Similar scores and frequencies are observed for different pair of source-target languages. In addition, it is worth noting that we observe comparable behaviour when scores are computed depending on the PoS of the tokens. Frequencies are relatively well preserved and the loss in UAS is shared among the PoS tags.

4 Conclusion

We have proposed to apply a simple method that learns transferred dependency parsers from partially projected data with the aim of analyzing the various parameters that impact the parsing performance. Our observations are valid for many methods of dependency transfer that operates on annotations (partially) projected via alignments links.

We have shown that the selection of the align-

label	frequencies (%)			UAS (%)		
	parsed		tr.	sup.		tr.
	fr	en	fr	en	fr	fr
adpmod	14.5	10.9	9.9	83.5	78.8	70.0
adpobj	13.2	10.7	9.8	95.4	92.2	85.1
det	13.3	10.4	12.9	96.9	96.6	95.3
nsubj	6.2	7.1	8.8	90.4	88.3	81.8
amod	6.0	5.9	6.7	94.1	92.1	88.2
root	3.3	3.6	8.4	89.8	78.0	71.3
dobj	4.9	4.2	4.8	92.4	91.6	86.2
advmod	3.4	4.3	4.2	83.5	74.2	71.5
conj	3.3	3.3	2.8	69.7	57.3	49.5
cc	2.7	3.2	2.8	75.2	62.9	54.3

Table 3: English-to-French transfer scores per dependency label and frequencies of these labels in the Europarl corpus, parsed and transferred (tr.). Supervised (sup.) scores for the source and target languages are also reported.

ments (thus the dependencies) and the filtering of the projected data are crucial. The quantity of projected data used for learning is not relevant if quality is not controlled. However, the quantity of training data is correlated to the parsing performance, as quantity is rather a consequence of the quality of the alignments. Finally, the quality of alignment greatly depends on the relation shared between the source and target languages. It appear that all these choices are far more important that the quality of the source parsing.

Moreover, we have seen that performance of transfer techniques still lag behind those of fully supervised learning. Our experiments suggest that many attachment errors are produced during the dependency projection and that these errors are spread over all kind of syntactic phenomena. They surely derived from alignment errors and variation in the annotation scheme between languages. The recent development of more coherent annotation schemes and corpora (universal dependencies (Nivre et al., 2015)) tends to alleviate these problems but there is still work to be done concerning the quality of the alignments. The main difficulty is to preserve enough sentences for learning while preventing the projection of erroneous dependencies.

---

[10]We are only considering the most frequent labels. The frequency of all ignored labels is less than 1%.

Acknowledgments

This work has been partly funded by a DGA-RAPID project under grant agreement N.º1429060465 (Papyrus). We thank the reviewers for their accurate comments and suggestions.

References

Lauriane Aufrant and Guillaume Wisniewski. 2016. PanParser: a Modular Implementation for Efficient Transition-Based Dependency Parsing. Technical report, LIMSI-CNRS, March.

Bernd Bohnet and Joakim Nivre. 2012. A transition-based system for joint part-of-speech tagging and labeled non-projective dependency parsing. In *Proceedings of the 2012 Joint Conference on Empirical Methods in Natural Language Processing and Computational Natural Language Learning*, pages 1455–1465, Jeju Island, Korea, July. Association for Computational Linguistics.

Shay B. Cohen, Dipanjan Das, and Noah A. Smith. 2011. Unsupervised Structure Prediction with Non-Parallel Multilingual Guidance. In *Proceedings of EMNLP 2011, the Conference on Empirical Methods in Natural Language Processing*, pages 50–61, Edinburgh, Scotland, UK., July.

Yoav Goldberg and Joakim Nivre. 2012. A Dynamic Oracle for Arc-Eager Dependency Parsing. In *Proceedings of COLING 2012, the International Conference on Computational Linguistics*, pages 959–976, Bombay, India.

Rebecca Hwa, Philip Resnik, A.Weinberg, C. Cabezas, and O. Kolak. 2005. Bootstrapping Parsers via Syntactic Projection accross Parallel Texts. *Natural language engineering*, 11:311–325.

Terry Koo, Xavier Carreras Pérez, and Michael Collins. 2008. Simple Semi-supervised Dependency Parsing. In *Proceedings of the 46th Annual Meeting of the Association for Computational Linguistics*, pages 595–603.

Ophélie Lacroix, Lauriane Aufrant, Guillaume Wisniewski, and François Yvon. 2016. Frustratingly easy cross-lingual transfer for transition-based dependency parsing. In *The 15th Annual Conference of the North American Chapter of the Association for Computational Linguistics: Human Language Technologies*, NAACL 2016, San Diego, California, USA.

Zhenghua Li, Min Zhang, and Wenliang Chen. 2014. Soft Cross-lingual Syntax Projection for Dependency Parsing. In *Proceedings of COLING 2014, the 25th International Conference on Computational Linguistics: Technical Papers*, pages 783–793, Dublin, Ireland. Dublin City University and Association for Computational Linguistics.

Xuezhe Ma and Fei Xia. 2014. Unsupervised dependency parsing with transferring distribution via parallel guidance and entropy regularization. In *Proceedings of the 52nd Annual Meeting of the Association for Computational Linguistics (Volume 1: Long Papers)*, pages 1337–1348, Baltimore, Maryland, June.

David Mareček. 2011. Combining Diverse Word-Alignment Symmetrizations Improves Dependency Tree Projection. In *Computational Linguistics and Intelligent Text Processing*, pages 144–154. Springer.

Ryan McDonald, Slav Petrov, and Keith Hall. 2011. Multi-source Transfer of Delexicalized Dependency Parsers. In *Proceedings of EMNLP 2011, the Conference on Empirical Methods in Natural Language Processing*, pages 62–72.

Ryan McDonald, Joakim Nivre, Yvonne Quirmbach-Brundage, Yoav Goldberg, Dipanjan Das, Kuzman Ganchev, Keith Hall, Slav Petrov, Hao Zhang, Oscar Täckström, Claudia Bedini, Núria Bertomeu Castelló, and Jungmee Lee. 2013. Universal Dependency Annotation for Multilingual Parsing. In *Proceedings of ACL 2013, the 51st Annual Meeting of the Association for Computational Linguistics (Volume 2: Short Papers)*, pages 92–97, Sofia, Bulgaria, August.

Tahira Naseem, Harr Chen, Regina Barzilay, and Mark Johnson. 2010. Using Universal Linguistic Knowledge to Guide Grammar Induction. In *Proceedings of EMNLP 2010, the Conference on Empirical Methods in Natural Language Processing*, pages 1234–1244, Stroudsburg, PA, USA.

Joakim Nivre, Željko Agić, Maria Jesus Aranzabe, Masayuki Asahara, Aitziber Atutxa, Miguel Ballesteros, John Bauer, Kepa Bengoetxea, Riyaz Ahmad Bhat, Cristina Bosco, Sam Bowman, Giuseppe G. A. Celano, Miriam Connor, Marie-Catherine de Marneffe, Arantza Diaz de Ilarraza, Kaja Dobrovoljc, Timothy Dozat, Tomaž Erjavec, Richárd Farkas, Jennifer Foster, Daniel Galbraith, Filip Ginter, Iakes Goenaga, Koldo Gojenola, Yoav Goldberg, Berta Gonzales, Bruno Guillaume, Jan Hajič, Dag Haug, Radu Ion, Elena Irimia, Anders Johannsen, Hiroshi Kanayama, Jenna Kanerva, Simon Krek, Veronika Laippala, Alessandro Lenci, Nikola Ljubešić, Teresa Lynn, Christopher Manning, Ctlina Mrnduc, David Mareček, Héctor Martínez Alonso, Jan Mašek, Yuji Matsumoto, Ryan McDonald, Anna Missilä, Verginica Mititelu, Yusuke Miyao, Simonetta Montemagni, Shunsuke Mori, Hanna Nurmi, Petya Osenova, Lilja Øvrelid, Elena Pascual, Marco Passarotti, Cenel-Augusto Perez, Slav Petrov, Jussi Piitulainen, Barbara Plank, Martin Popel, Prokopis Prokopidis, Sampo Pyysalo, Loganathan Ramasamy,

Rudolf Rosa, Shadi Saleh, Sebastian Schuster, Wolfgang Seeker, Mojgan Seraji, Natalia Silveira, Maria Simi, Radu Simionescu, Katalin Simkó, Kiril Simov, Aaron Smith, Jan Štěpánek, Alane Suhr, Zsolt Szántó, Takaaki Tanaka, Reut Tsarfaty, Sumire Uematsu, Larraitz Uria, Viktor Varga, Veronika Vincze, Zdeněk Žabokrtský, Daniel Zeman, and Hanzhi Zhu. 2015. Universal dependencies 1.2. LINDAT/CLARIN digital library at Institute of Formal and Applied Linguistics, Charles University in Prague.

Joakim Nivre. 2003. An Efficient Algorithm for Projective Dependency Parsing. In *Proceedings of IWPT 2003, the 8th International Workshop on Parsing Technologies*, Nancy, France.

Franz Joseph Och and Hermann Ney. 2003. A systematic comparison of various statistical alignment models. *Computational Linguistics*, 29:19–51.

Mohammad Sadegh Rasooli and Michael Collins. 2015. Density-driven cross-lingual transfer of dependency parsers. In *Proceedings of the 2015 Conference on Empirical Methods in Natural Language Processing*, pages 328–338, Lisbon, Portugal, September. Association for Computational Linguistics.

Anders Søgaard. 2011. Data point selection for cross-language adaptation of dependency parsers. In *Proceedings of ACL 2011, the 49th Annual Meeting of the Association for Computational Linguistics: Human Language Technologies*, pages 682–686, Portland, Oregon, USA, June.

Kathrin Spreyer and Jonas Kuhn. 2009. Data-Driven Dependency Parsing of New Languages Using Incomplete and Noisy Training Data. In *Proceedings of CoNLL 2009, the Thirteenth Conference on Computational Natural Language Learning*, pages 12–20, Boulder, Colorado, June.

Oscar Täckström, Ryan McDonald, and Joakim Nivre. 2013. Target Language Adaptation of Discriminative Transfer Parsers. In *Proceedings of ACL 2013, the Conference of the North American Chapter of the Association for Computational Linguistics: Human Language Technologies*, pages 1061–1071, Atlanta, Georgia.

Jörg Tiedemann. 2014. Rediscovering Annotation Projection for Cross-Lingual Parser Induction. In *Proceedings of COLING 2014, the 25th International Conference on Computational Linguistics: Technical Papers*, pages 1854–1864, Dublin, Ireland, August. Dublin City University and Association for Computational Linguistics.

Guillaume Wisniewski, Nicolas Pécheux, Souhir Gahbiche-Braham, and François Yvon. 2014. Cross-lingual part-of-speech tagging through ambiguous learning. In *Proceedings of the 2014 Conference on Empirical Methods in Natural Language Processing (EMNLP)*, pages 1779–1785, Doha, Qatar, October.

Daniel Zeman and Philip Resnik. 2008. Cross-Language Parser Adaptation between Related Languages. In *Proceedings of the IJCNLP-08 Workshop on NLP for Less Privileged Languages*, pages 35–42, Hyderabad, India, January. Asian Federation of Natural Language Processing.

Yue Zhang and Joakim Nivre. 2011. Transition-based Dependency Parsing with Rich Non-local Features. In *Proceedings of ACL 2011, the 49th Annual Meeting of the Association for Computational Linguistics: Human Language Technologies*, pages 188–193, Portland, Oregon, USA, June. Association for Computational Linguistics.

Yue Zhang and Joakim Nivre. 2012. Analyzing the Effect of Global Learning and Beam-Search on Transition-Based Dependency Parsing. In *Proceedings of COLING 2012, the 24th International Conference on Computational Linguistics: Technical Papers*, pages 1391–1400, Mumbai, India, December.

Enhancing Automatic Wordnet Construction Using Word Embeddings

Feras Al Tarouti
University of Colorado Colorado Springs
1420 Austin Bluffs Pkwy
Colorado Springs, CO 80918, USA
faltarou@uccs.edu

Jugal Kalita
University of Colorado Colorado Springs
1420 Austin Bluffs Pkwy
Colorado Springs, CO 80918, USA
jkalita@uccs.edu

Abstract

Researchers have shown that a wordnet for a new language, possibly resource-poor, can be constructed automatically by translating wordnets of resource-rich languages. The quality of these constructed wordnets is affected by the quality of the resources used such as dictionaries and translation methods in the construction process. Recent work shows that vector representation of words (word embeddings) can be used to discover related words in text. In this paper, we propose a method that performs such similarity computation using word embeddings to improve the quality of automatically constructed wordnets.

1 Introduction

A wordnet is a lexical ontology of words. High-quality wordnets have been developed for only a few languages. Wordnets, other than the Princeton WordNet (PWN) (Fellbaum, 1998), are typically constructed by one of two approaches. The translation approach translates the PWN to target languages (Saveski and Trajkovski, 2010; Oliver and Climent, 2012; Lam et al., 2014). In contrast, the merge approach builds the semantic taxonomy of a wordnet in a target language, and then aligns it with the Princeton WordNet by generating translations (Gunawan and Saputra, 2010; Rodríguez et al., 2008).

In this paper, we propose a method to enhance the translation approach using word embeddings produced by the *word2vec* algorithm (Mikolov et al., 2013). We produce wordnets in several languages

although the current paper focuses only on the new Arabic wordnet we construct.

2 Constructing Initial Wordnet

We start by automatically generating wordnet synsets for a target language T using the method presented by (Lam et al., 2014), which translates synsets from several intermediate wordnets and ranks them. The approach generates wordnet synsets that do not include any semantic links between them. This paper discusses how we construct the semantic links between synsets in T. Figure 1 shows that we take advantage of the fact that the wordnet synsets created in the previous step are aligned with PWN. This means that synsets with the same meaning for different languages share the same synset ID. To construct the links between synsets in our new wordnet TWN for language T, we extract each $synset_i^{TWN}$ from TWN and find the corresponding synset in PWN, $synset_i^{PWN}$. Here, i is the ID of the synset. Then, for each $synset_i^{PWN}$, we extract each semantic relations r_j and all linked $synset_k^{PWN}$ within PWN. Finally, if $synset_k$, i.e., a synset with ID k is present in TWN, we add a link between $synset_i^{TWN}$ and $synset_k^{TWN}$ in the newly constructed TWN.

3 Generating Word Embeddings

In order to validate the synsets we create using translation and obtain relations between them, we use the *word2vec* algorithm (Mikolov et al., 2013) to generate word representations from an existing corpus. The *word2vec* algorithm uses a feedforward neural network to predict the vector representation of

30

Proceedings of the Workshop on Multilingual and Cross-lingual Methods in NLP, pages 30–34,
San Diego, California, June 17, 2016. ©2016 Association for Computational Linguistics

Pair	Cosine Similarity
$(word_1, word_2)$	0.91
$(word_1, word_3)$	0.22
$(word_1, word_4)$	0.82
$(word_2, word_3)$	0.34
$(word_2, word_4)$	0.72
$(word_3, word_4)$	0.12

Table 1: An example of cosine similarity between words in a candidate synset

words within a multi-dimensional language model. $Word2vec$ has two variations: Skip-Gram (SG) and Continuous Bag-Of-Words (CBOW). In the SG version, the neural network predicts words adjacent to a given word on either side, while in the CBOW model the network predicts the word in the middle of a given sequence of words. In the work presented in this paper, we generate representations of words using both models with several different vector and window sizes to obtain the settings for the highest precision. The purpose of the steps discussed next is to improve the quality of synsets produced by the translation process in addition to generating relations among the synsets.

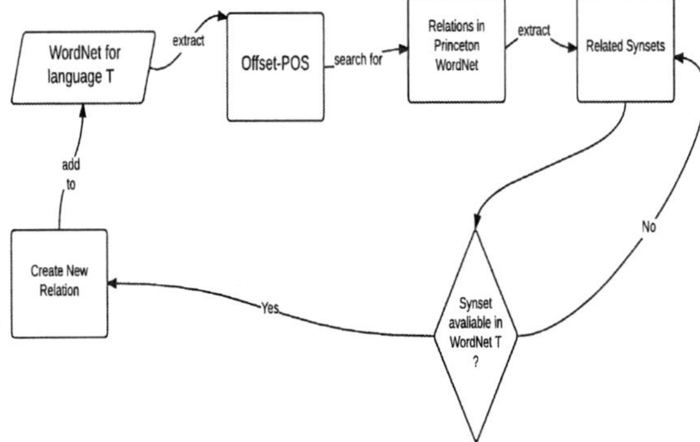

Figure 1: Creating wordnet semantic relations using intermediate wordnet.

3.1 Removing irrelevant words in synsets

We compute the cosine similarity between word vectors within each single synset in TWN, the wordnet being constructed in language T, to filter false word members within synsets. To filter the initially constructed synsets in TWN, we pick a threshold value α such that the selected words have cosine similarity larger than α with each other. For example, let $synset_i^c = \{word_1, word_2, word_3, word_4\}$

be a candidate synset to be potentially included in TWN. We compute the cosine similarity between all the possible pairs of words in $synset_i^c$. Then, we extract the pair of words with the highest cosine similarity. If this pair of words have cosine similarity larger than α, the pair is kept in the final synset $synset_i$, otherwise, $synset_i^c$ itself is discarded. This may have been a low quality candidate synset generated in the translation process. Next, among the remaining words in $synset_i^c$, a word is kept if it has a connection with any word in $synset_i$ with similarity higher than α. For example, let us assume that the cosine similarity between the words in $synset_i^c$ are as shown in Table 1 and α=0.70. First, the pair with the highest cosine similarity, $(word_1, word_2)$ is kept in the final $synset_i$ since its cosine similarity is larger than α. Then, $word_3$ is discarded since it does not have any cosine similarity larger than α with any of the words in the current final $synset_i$. Finally, $word_4$ is kept $synset_i$ since it does have a cosine similarity with $word_1$ that satisfies the threshold α.

3.2 Validating candidate relations

Similarly, we compute the cosine similarity between words within pairs of semantically related synsets. This allow us to verify the constructed relations between synsets in TWN. For example, let $synset_i = \{word_{i1}, word_{i2}, word_{i3}, word_{i4}\}$, $synset_j = \{word_{j1}, word_{j2}, word_{j3}, word_{j4}\}$ be synsets in TWN. And let ρ_{ij} be a candidate semantic relation between $synset_i$ and $synset_j$. We compute the cosine similarity between all the possible pairs of words from $synset_i$ to $synset_j$ and obtain the maximum similarity obtained. Then, if this value is larger than a threshold α_ρ, then we retain the relation ρ_{ij}, otherwise, we discard it.

3.3 Selecting thresholds

To pick the synset similarity threshold value α and the threshold α_ρ for each semantic relation we create, we compute the cosine similarity between pairs of synonym words, semantically related words, and non-related words obtained from existing wordnets. Then, based on the previous data, we select the threshold values that are associated with higher precision and maximum coverage.

4 Experiments

We discuss the generation of a wordnet for Arabic as an example although we have worked with several other languages.

4.1 Datasets and Resources Used

To construct the core wordnet, i.e., wordnet synsets, we use the Microsoft Translator to translate English synsets from PWN to Arabic synsets. We have selected the Microsoft Translator because it gives acceptable quality free of cost. For generating vector representations of the Arabic Words we use the following freely available corpora: Watan-2004 corpus (12 million words) (Abbas et al., 2011), Khaleej-2004 corpus (3 million) (Abbas and Smaili, 2005) and 21 million words of Wikipedia[1] Arabic articles, combined to a single file.

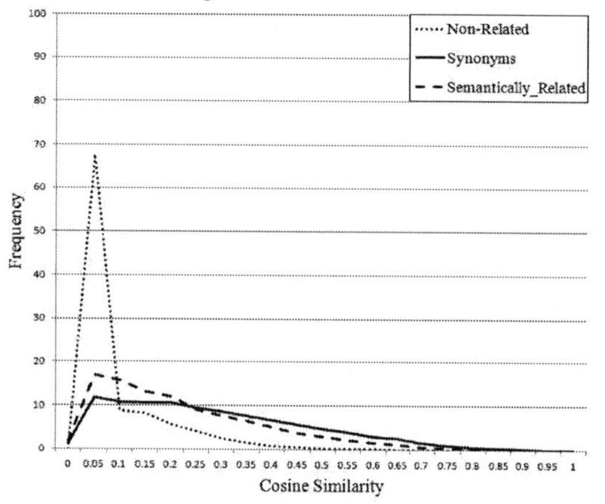

Figure 2: A histogram of synonyms, semantically related words, and non-related words extracted from AWN.

In order to compute the synset similarity threshold value α and the threshold for each semantic relation α_ρ, we use the freely available Arabic wordnet (AWN) (Rodríguez et al., 2008). AWN was manually constructed in 2006 and has been semi-automatically enhanced and extended several times. We start by extracting synonym words, semantically related words, and non-related words from AWN. Then, we use the histogram representation of the cosine similarity of the previous sets of words to set the thresholds. As Figure 2 shows, more than 67% of the non-related words have cosine similarity less than 0.1, while about 23% of the synonym words in

---

[1] https://ar.wikipedia.org

Relation	Weighted Average Similarity
Synonyms	0.28
Hypernyms	0.22
TopicDomains	0.23
PartHolonyms	0.28
InstanceHypernyms	0.08
MemberMeronyms	0.29

Table 2: The weighted average similarity between related words in AWN.

Relation	Count
Hypernyms	55,336
MemberMeronyms	11,408
SimilarTo	10,826
PartHolonyms	7,051
TopicDomains	3,863

Table 3: Number of Arabic synset relations we create.

AWN have a cosine similarity less than 0.1. Furthermore, about 34% of the semantically related words in AWN have cosine similarity less than 0.1. Table 2 shows the weighted average cosine similarity between synonyms, hypernyms, topic-domain related, part-holonyms, instance-hypernyms, and member-meronyms in AWN where the frequency of the similarity value is the weight.

4.2 Creating an Arabic Wordnet

We choose the algorithm for creating wordnet synsets presented by (Lam et al., 2014) because it requires a limited number of freely available resources, which makes it applicable to resource-poor languages. Then, we apply the method we propose in Section 2 to create semantic links between Arabic synsets. Table 3 shows statistics of some of the created links between synsets in our Arabic wordnet.

4.3 Producing Word Embeddings for Arabic

We test the $word2vec$ algorithm with different window sizes. We generate word embeddings using the CBOW version with window sizes 3, 5 and 8. Next, we compute the weighted averages of the cosine similarity between the synonyms in AWN. The highest weighted average we obtained was 0.288 with window size 3, while the weighted averages obtained with window sizes 5 and 8 were 0.283 and

Algorithm	Vector Size	Similarity Average
SG	100	0.289
SG	200	0.258
SG	500	0.194
CBOW	100	0.288
CBOW	200	0.259
CBOW	500	0.195

Table 4: Comparison between the weighted similarity average obtained using different $word2vec$ settings.

Threshold	AWN	Our Arabic WordNet
0.000	5,941	17,349
0.100	3,433	2,073
0.288	2,471	943
0.500	1,190	271
0.750	209	13

Table 5: Comparison between the number of synsets in AWN and our Arabic wordnet using different threshold values.

	Threshold Range		
	0- 0.1	0.1 - 0.288	0.288 - 1
Synonyms	34.8%	56.8%	78.4%
Hypernyms	45.2%	57.2%	84.4%
PartHolonym	50.8%	75.2%	90.4%
Member-Meronym	40.8%	56.8%	79.6%

Table 6: Precision of the Arabic wordnet we create.

0.277 respectively. Then, we compare between the SG and the CBOW with different vector sizes. Table 4 shows the weighted average cosine similarity obtained between $16,000$ pairs of synonyms in AWN using both variations of $word2vec$, with window size=3 and vector size set to 100, 200, and 500. We notice that both versions produce almost similar results with a slight advantage to SG with the cost of more execution time. However, for the corpus we use, smaller vector size produces better precision.

4.4 Evaluation & Discussion

We compute cosine similarity between semantically related words extracted from our initial Arabic wordnet produced in Section 4.2. The language model to calculate the cosine similarity is created using CBOW with vector size=100 and window size=3. Table 5 shows a comparison between the number of Arabic synsets we create and the number of synsets in AWN.

We notice that the translation method we use produces high number of synsets compared to the manually constructed AWN. However, the number of synsets sharply decreases after filtering the initial synonyms using the method described in Section 3. Although our Arabic wordnet is automatically created, the number of synsets we create is 60% of the number of synsets in the manually created AWN

when filtering the synsets using $\alpha = 0.1$.

We evaluate precision by comparing 600 pairs of synonyms, hypernyms, part-holonyms, and member-meronyms with three ranges of cosine similarity values: 0 to 0.1, 0.1 to 0.288, and 0.288 to 1. We asked 3 Arabic speakers to evaluate the pairs using a 0 to 5 scale where 0 represents the minimum score and 5 represents the maximum score. We compute precision by taking the average score and converting it to a percentage. See Table 6.

The precision of the synonyms, hypernyms, part-holonyms, and member-meronyms we produce is 78.4%, 84.4%, 90.4%, and 79.6% respectively, with the threshold set to 0.288. This is higher than the precision obtained by (Lam et al., 2014) which produces synonyms with 76.4% precision when just using PWN. Our results suggest that using lower precision for producing synsets reduces the quality of the other created semantic relations. Our results clearly show that pairs with higher cosine similarity are more likely to be semantically related. It confirms the benefit of combining the translation method with word embeddings in the process of automatically generating new wordnets.

5 Conclusion & Future Work

In this paper, we discuss an approach for automatically generating new wordnets for low-resource languages. Our approach takes advantage of word embeddings to enhance the translation method for automatic wordnet creation. We present an application of our approach to producing new Arabic Wordnet. Our method automatically produces Arabic synonyms with 78.4% precision and semantically related pairs of words with up to 90.4% precision. Currently, we are in the process of applying our method to other languages such as Assamese, Bengali and Tamil.

References

Mourad Abbas and Kamel Smaili. 2005. Comparison of topic identification methods for arabic language. In *International Conference on Recent Advances in Natural Language Processing-RANLP 2005*, volume 14.

Mourad Abbas, Kamel Smaïli, and Daoud Berkani. 2011. Evaluation of topic identification methods on arabic corpora. *JDIM*, 9(5):185–192.

Christiane Fellbaum. 1998. *Wordnet: An electronic lexical database*. MIT Press Cambridge.

G Gunawan and Andy Saputra. 2010. Building synsets for Indonesian Wordnet with monolingual lexical resources. In *Asian Language Processing (IALP), 2010 International Conference on*, pages 297–300. IEEE.

Khang Nhut Lam, Feras A. Tarouti, and Jugal Kalita. 2014. Automatically constructing wordnet synsets. In *52nd Annual Meeting of the Association for Computational Linguistics (ACL 2014), Baltimore, USA, June*.

Tomas Mikolov, Wen-tau Yih, and Geoffrey Zweig. 2013. Linguistic regularities in continuous space word representations. In *HLT-NAACL*, pages 746–751.

Antoni Oliver and Salvador Climent. 2012. Parallel corpora for wordnet construction: Machine translation vs. automatic sense tagging. In *Computational Linguistics and Intelligent Text Processing*, pages 110–121. Springer.

Horacio Rodríguez, David Farwell, Javi Ferreres, Manuel Bertran, Musa Alkhalifa, and Maria Antònia Martí. 2008. Arabic wordnet: Semi-automatic extensions using bayesian inference. In *LREC*.

Martin Saveski and Igor Trajkovski. 2010. Automatic construction of wordnets by using machine translation and language modeling. In *13th Multiconference Information Society, Ljubljana, Slovenia*.

Cross-lingual alignment transfer: a chicken-and-egg story?

Lauriane Aufrant[1,2] and **Guillaume Wisniewski**[1] and **François Yvon**[1]
[1] LIMSI, CNRS, Univ. Paris-Sud, Université Paris-Saclay, 91 403 Orsay, France
[2]DGA, 60 boulevard du Général Martial Valin, 75 509 Paris, France
`{lauriane.aufrant,guillaume.wisniewski,francois.yvon}@limsi.fr`

Abstract

In this paper, we challenge a basic assumption of many cross-lingual transfer techniques: the availability of word aligned parallel corpora, and consider ways to accommodate situations in which such resources do not exist. We show experimentally that, here again, weakly supervised cross-lingual learning techniques can prove useful, once adapted to transfer knowledge *across pairs of languages*.

1 Introduction

Supervised machine learning techniques lie at the core of many robust Natural Language Processing (NLP) systems and components. The dissemination of such methodologies is however hindered by the lack of appropriate supervision data, which are costly to produce and only available for a restricted number of genres, tasks, domains and languages. *Weakly supervised learning* techniques have emerged as an effective way to remedy, at least partially, to this unsatisfactory situation. Among them, *cross-lingual learning methods* enable to transfer useful supervision information from well-resourced to under-resourced languages, speeding up the development of NLP tools for new domains and tasks.

Many techniques for transferring knowledge across languages have been proposed in the literature (see § 2 for a brief overview). A widely-used methodology consists in generating automatic annotations for the resource-poor language by projecting linguistic information through word alignment links (see eg. (Yarowsky et al., 2001; Täckström et al., 2013) for PoS tagging, (Hwa et al., 2005;

Lacroix et al., 2016a) for dependency parsing, (Ehrmann et al., 2011) for Named Entity Recognition, (Kozhevnikov and Titov, 2013) for Semantic Role Labeling, etc.). Implementing this methodology requires the existence of (a) parallel corpora aligned at the word level, and (b) annotation and/or tools on the resource-rich side. However, requirement (a) is somewhat paradoxical: reliable word alignments can only be computed for large-scale parallel corpora, a situation that is unlikely to happen for actual under-resourced languages.

In this study, we explore ways to overcome this paradox and consider techniques for *transferring alignment models or annotations across language pairs*, a task that has hardly been addressed in literature (see however (Wang et al., 2006; Levinboim and Chiang, 2015)). Based on a high-level typology of cross-lingual transfer methodologies (§ 2), our contribution is to formalize realistic scenarios (defined in § 3) as well as some basic methodologies for projecting knowledge about bilingual alignments cross-linguistically (§ 4). Experiments in § 5 show that, at least for some of these scenarios, simple-minded methods can be surprisingly effective and open a discussion on further prospects and perspectives for future work.

2 Techniques for cross-lingual transfer

In this section, we briefly review existing cross-lingual transfer techniques for various NLP applications, aiming at identifying techniques that could be adapted for transferring alignments. We will successively consider techniques that operate in the data space, then techniques that perform the transfer of

35

Proceedings of the Workshop on Multilingual and Cross-lingual Methods in NLP, pages 35–44,
San Diego, California, June 17, 2016. ©2016 Association for Computational Linguistics

parameters. Note that for the sake of the presentation, the resource-rich is viewed as the source language, and the resource-poor is accordingly the target language.

2.1 Transfer in data space

This family of techniques seeks to automatically supply the annotations that are lacking on the target side, so that a model can be learned on these artificially generated data.

Direct Transfer Two main lines of reasoning have been considered: the first assumes that the source and target languages are sufficiently similar, to the point that source annotations can be readily used to train a model in the target language (Hana et al., 2004; Zeman and Resnik, 2008). When such assumption does not hold, a necessary preliminary step will be to map the source and target data in a shared representation space: *delexicalization*, i.e. the replacement of words with (universal) PoS (McDonald et al., 2013) readily yields such mappings (Wisniewski et al., 2014), but it is also conceivable to consider automatically inferred multilingual representations (Jagarlamudi et al., 2011; Kočiský et al., 2014; Gouws et al., 2015). This simple approach has one downside: learning can only use features based on this inter-lingual representation – in particular this makes it impossible to include powerful lexical features. Delexicalized training thus needs to be complemented by a relexicalization phase, where more informative features can then come into play (McDonald et al., 2011). In fact, in this situation, transfer is nothing but a specific case of domain adaptation (Blitzer, 2008), and can be handled with the same tools (semi-supervised learning, instance re-weighting, etc).

Annotation Projection The alternative is to preserve the lexical representations in each language, which are matched through word alignment in a parallel corpus. As mentioned above, this approach has been successful for many tasks. A very strong assumption is that words (or structures) that are mutual translations will carry identical annotations: this only holds for a restricted number of annotations and languages. For instance, it is commonly assumed that coarse-grained morphosyntactic tags can reasonably be projected between most West-European languages; such projections are less appropriate for fine-grained morphological information such as case or gender (as those distinctions greatly vary across languages), and would be even less so for pairs of languages having antagonist definitions of a word. Furthermore, its success will depend on the density and quality of the alignments (Lacroix et al., 2016b), meaning that it might be more suited to situations in which large bitexts are available. A possible workaround to the noisiness issue is to interpret transferred annotations as soft, rather than hard constraints: see e.g. (Ganchev et al., 2009; Das and Petrov, 2011; Li et al., 2014; Wang and Manning, 2014) for various implementations of this idea; or to combine it with another source of information (Täckström et al., 2013). Alignment projection is not only noisy: it also yields *incomplete annotations*, requiring methods that learn from partially annotated corpora (Wisniewski et al., 2014). A last strategy worth mentioning here for generating artificial annotations is to use Machine Translation (Tiedemann, 2014).

2.2 Transfer in parameter space

The second main family of techniques *use the same model for the source and target languages*: learned parameters in the former can then readily be used for the latter.

A first instance of model transfer has already been mentioned: indeed, taking source annotations to supervise the training in target can also be viewed as a (trivial) form of direct model transfer. This approach has been extended in many ways. Cohen et al. (2011) use several source languages and train one delexicalized model in each; the optimal convex combination of these models is used to process the target language. A variant of this strategy is to view the source parameter values as priors for the target model, an idea that has been used repeatedly in the context of domain adaptation. It has notably been used for transferring parsers (Cohen and Smith, 2009; Burkett et al., 2010; Berg-Kirkpatrick and Klein, 2010) and, more recently, to also transfer alignment models (Levinboim and Chiang, 2015).

This brief retrospective has demonstrated the variety of cross-lingual transfer techniques, many of which are borrowed from the domain adaptation literature. The applicability and success of these methods depend on the task and of the available resources. We now explore ways to apply them for the word alignment task.

3 Word alignments: cross-lingual scenarios

After a quick review of standard algorithms for word alignment, we present situations in which they can be improved by cross-lingual knowledge.

3.1 Aligning words

The most popular models for statistical word alignment are the IBM models 1 to 6 (Brown et al., 1993; Och and Ney, 2003) and the HMM model of Vogel et al. (1996). These probabilistic generative models decompose the probability of an aligned sentence pair as the conjunction of a word translation model, a distortion model (models 2 and up) and a fertility model (models 3 and up). Distortion is absolute for models 2-3 and relative for models 4-6; in the HMM model, it is captured by Markovian dependencies between consecutive alignments links. Among these parameters, the translation model is lexicalized in both languages, fertility is lexicalized in the source side and distortion is unlexicalized but rely on word clusters for models 4-6. In all cases, parameters are learned in an unsupervised way using the EM algorithm.

Many refinements to these algorithms have been proposed, often to improve computational performance (Dyer et al., 2013). Another line of work tries to improve IBM and HMM models' low generalization power by using feature-based models (Moore, 2005; Berg-Kirkpatrick et al., 2010). However, the IBM models remain today the most widely used approach both because of their efficiency and because they do not require any annotated data. They will thus serve as our main baseline.

3.2 Real-world situations for alignment transfer

Scenarios for improving word alignment with cross-lingual transfer fall into two categories, depending on whether the source and target languages play a symmetric role.

We first consider the standard symmetric BRIDGE scenario: it involves two languages S and T, for which large bitexts with a 'bridge' language B exist, readily yielding reasonably-good alignment models for S-B and B-T. We are however specifically interested in the S-T pair, for which we only possess a small parallel corpus. This can happen either in the context of a bilingual task like translation or because word alignments are needed for cross-lingual transfer of a monolingual model. In this case, the purpose is to annotate the S-T data thanks to information contained in the high quality S-B and B-T models. Two variants provide interesting refinement opportunities: MULTIPARALLEL, in which part or all the S-T parallel data is also aligned with sentences in B, and RELATED, when all three languages belong to the same linguistic family. Taking advantage of such similarity however requires more expressive models than the IBM series, which only operate at the level of word forms and are therefore agnostic to lexical similarities.

We can illustrate the RELATED scenario on the example of morphosyntactic model transfer from Italian (it) to Romanian (ro), using annotation projection. For lack of a large it:ro corpus to compute robust word alignments, an option is to use French as a bridge, collect large bitexts for Italian-French and for French-Romanian, and improve the quality of the Italian-Romanian word alignment model thanks to the it:fr and fr:ro models. Even though the resulting it:ro bitext is noisier and smaller than the fr:ro one, which could also be used for transferring PoS labels, transfer to Romanian may still be more accurate when using Italian as an additional source, or even as a better source than French.

In the second type of scenarios, source and target languages play asymmetric roles. Bitexts for S-T (eg. English and Ukrainian) come with small parallel data, but there exists a language $\tilde{T}$ related to T (and unrelated to S) for which large parallel data with S are available (eg. Russian). We consequently consider transfer of S-$\tilde{T}$ word alignments to the S-T pair. This can be interpreted as standard cross-lingual transfer from $\tilde{T}$ to T, but with the difference that the transferred knowledge is not monolingual but bilingual because of the interactions with S. With large data in both S-$\tilde{T}$ and $\tilde{T}$-T, we call this scenario DIRECTED BRIDGE. This is for instance the context of Wang et al. (2006)'s works on English-Japanese, using Chinese as a bridge language, but their cross-language word similarity does not exploit Chinese-Japanese linguistic similarity.

Finally, in the DIALECT scenario, T is a dialect of $\tilde{T}$, and even though parallel $\tilde{T}$-T data is not necessarily available, the transfer process can rely on the large number of common word forms. This would, for instance, be the case with the alignment of English with MS Arabic and dialects. Thanks to the large linguistic overlap, and contrarily to the previous scenarios, here again methods from the domain adaptation literature (Hua et al., 2005) may also successfully apply.

Before closing this section, we would finally like to stress the fact that the motivations for transferring alignments can be many: one might want to get alignments for a small parallel bitext, to then transfer other annotations, or one might want to bootstrap an alignment model with transferred parameters, or even to train a small SMT, etc. Each such motivation may call for different strategies.

4   Methods for transferring alignment

In this section, we exemplify with simple systems how general transfer methods can be instantiated for alignment transfer.

From now on, we focus on a DIRECTED BRIDGE scenario, further assuming that the task is to annotate a very small parallel corpus. We will simulate this situation, in Section 5, for the English-Swedish pair and choose Danish as a bridge language, as it is closely related to Swedish. Both English-Danish and Danish-Swedish pairs will be considered well-resourced.

We start with a straightforward baseline (CAT-DA), consisting in concatenating the English-Danish and the English-Swedish data before training. The underlying assumption is that both Danish and Swedish are subsumed by a Scandinavian meta-language. Despite their similarity, these languages only have few common word forms (Zeman and Resnik, 2008) and their vocabularies overlap mostly on function words, numbers and proper nouns. Consequently, the resulting translation model will in fact consist in two quite separate sub-models that hardly interact. A unique model is however trained for the unlexicalized parameters like distortion.

This approach corresponds to joint learning with parameter sharing. It can however be interpreted from another point of view: as the purpose of transfer at the data level is to produce noisy artificial training data, here we produce approximate English-Swedish sentence pairs, with the Danish set considered as a proxy to Swedish.

We continue along these lines and propose a second method to produce fake Swedish data: first train an IBM 1 model on the Danish-Swedish corpus to extract a translation model, then replace every Danish token of the English-Danish data with its most likely translation (leaving OOV tokens unchanged). Then again the resulting bitext is concatenated with the English-Swedish corpus and standard training ensues. We notice that a symmetrical procedure can be straightforwardly implemented, by using a Swedish-Danish IBM 1 model to translate the test set in Danish: alignment is performed in the Danish domain, but since there is an exact Swedish-Danish token correspondence, the resulting word alignment can be directly used for the English-Swedish part. This is an example where English-Swedish IBM models will not be delivered, and can hardly be re-estimated from so few sentence pairs. We denote these methods TR-DA and DA-TR respectively.

The same intuitions can finally be applied for transferring in the parameter space: direct transfer is achieved by training an English-Danish model, then using it directly to annotate the English-Swedish pairs (E step of the EM algorithm). This approach (denoted DA) is rather naive and is expected to perform poorly, but it can be improved in a similar manner to the 'glosses' method of (Zeman and Resnik, 2008), by translating the Swedish tokens into Danish with a Swedish-Danish IBM 1 model (a method denoted GLOSSES-DA). Using the converse translation model to translate the English-Danish lexicalized model parameters and thus produce a full English-Swedish model yields slightly different results (PARAM-DA). The six methods are summarized in Table 1.

Deriving other methods   The purpose of those strategies is mostly to set baselines and qualitative analyses, and more complex alignment transfer methods can be designed, following the typology of § 2. Two restrictions apply however.

First, annotation projection can not be entertained

DATA SPACE		
CAT-L	concatenate en:L and test data; train	
TR-L	word-for-word translate en:L data; concatenate with test data; train	
L-TR	word-for-word translate test data in L; concatenate with en:L data; train	
PARAMETER SPACE		
L	train an en:L model; apply on test data	
GLOSSES-L	train an en:L model; apply on test data word-for-word translated in L	
PARAM-L	train an en:L model; translate the parameters; apply on test data	

Table 1: Summary of proposed methods, for bridge language L.

in any scenario: while annotation projection for a monolingual task needs parallel data, for a bilingual model it would require multiparallel data. The converse is not true however, and the MULTIPARALLEL scenario can be successfully exploited without annotation projection (Kumar et al., 2007).

Second, the delexicalized approach causes a chicken-and-egg situation in real-life scenarios. Indeed, when the target language is under-resourced, one cannot assume the availability of a PoS tagger that is needed to compute delexicalized representations. Conversely, methods like (Wisniewski et al., 2014)'s cross-lingual PoS tagger projection and (Täckström et al., 2012)'s clusters are not applicable without a word aligned corpus. Finding common, even coarse-grained, representations then becomes a huge obstacle in many scenarios where alignment transfer is needed, which makes this approach less relevant.

As a final note, we point out that the RELATED scenario can be simulated with two symmetric instances of DIRECTED BRIDGE interpolated in the data or parameter space. The straightforward strategies described here can therefore be extended to other scenarios.

5 Experiments

In this section, we experiment with the methods introduced above and compare them with standard unsupervised models of varying sizes.

Experimental setup We evaluate the proposed alignment transfer methods on the English-Swedish test set provided by Holmqvist and Ahrenberg (2011), which consists of 192 word aligned sentence pairs extracted from the English-Swedish part of Europarl (Koehn,). We score the methods according to the intrinsic Alignment Error Rate (AER) metric proposed by Och and Ney (2000).

As documented in a large body of literature (Lopez and Resnik, 2006; Fraser and Marcu, 2007; Lambert et al., 2009; Lambert et al., 2010), AER poorly correlates with translation quality of the systems trained on the evaluated alignments, especially for large corpora, and extrinsic metrics like the BLEU score should be preferred, were MT training the final goal of alignment.

The concatenation methods proposed here are intended for very small data, with large unbalance between the target and the bridge sets, a data size for which the SMT application is not relevant. Consequently, we use the PoS accuracy of a cross-lingual tagger (Wisniewski et al., 2014) weakly supervised by the word alignments as the extrinsic evaluation metric of our methods. In such a system, each extra sentence pair brings valuable knowledge, while incorrect links strongly noise the system, making the accuracy a direct indicator of alignment quality. Besides, this step completes a realistic low-resource scenario where word alignments are needed for an intended cross-lingual use.

We use the English-Swedish bitext both as a test set for intrinsic evaluation and as projection data to train cross-lingual taggers. PoS accuracies are computed on the coarse PoS tags of the Swedish test treebank of the Universal Dependencies 1.2 (McDonald et al., 2013) and the source English tagger is trained on the training portion of the same corpus. In every method where additional parallel data is required, we use Europarl without the Q4-2000 section, which is reserved for tests.

We evaluate AER and PoS accuracy for the

three concatenation methods presented in § 4, with transfer through Danish: CAT-DA, TR-DA, DA-TR, and the three parameter transfer methods: DA, GLOSSES-DA, PARAM-DA. To evaluate the benefits of using a related bridge language, we also run the concatenation experiments with transfer through Greek, that is only distantly related to Swedish and also uses a different alphabet (methods CAT-EL, TR-EL, EL-TR). Finally, the alignment performance is confronted with that of concatenation with English-Swedish data of various sizes, from no added pair (BASELINE) to full concatenation of the 1.8M sentence pairs in Europarl (CAT-SV).

Results Table 2 reports the AERs of the various methods when using IBM 1, HMM or IBM 4 models. The methods involving test set translation (DA-TR and GLOSSES-DA) consistently yield the best cross-lingual accuracies for each model, with a relative error reduction of 45%, 52% and 59% respectively for DA-TR and scores comparable to the full English-Swedish ones. Figure 1 reports those AERs along the learning curves of English-Swedish models for increasing data sizes. It shows that the DA-TR method yields alignment quality comparable to unsupervised learning on 0.1M to 0.5M sentence pairs.

The PoS accuracy measures are reported in Table 3. They show a clear correlation of the most effective (in AER) transfer methods with high PoS accuracies. However, this measure does not allow to clearly rank the top few models (CAT-SV, TR-DA, DA-TR and GLOSSES-DA). Notably, here CAT-DA and DA-TR respectively outperform BASELINE and CAT-SV. It may be that word alignments obtained by transfer are less accurate but focus more on general cross-lingual structures which, in turn, enables a better annotation projection, or that these score differences are simply not significant. Coming up with a reliable interpretation of this issue however will require further experiments that are beyond the scope of this paper.

Discussion Unsurprisingly, direct data transfer methods CAT-DA and CAT-EL perform at best in par with the baseline, and often worse. Indeed, because of mostly disjoint vocabularies, the translation model is globally not improved by the external knowledge, while training the Swedish parameters on few pairs compared to the whole data pro-

duces weak parameters that are easily subject to any noise coming from the few common word forms (see IBM 1 results). This approach could however perform better in a DIALECT scenario, assuming that the $\tilde{T}$ and T languages have large enough common vocabularies to structure the alignment sets, and that shared word forms are not accidental but actually correspond to common words that can be reliably exploited to transfer knowledge. The absolute AER gap reduces when adding shared distortion and fertility models, but this does not allow us to conclude on a positive or negative effect of unlexicalized parameter sharing. This suggests however the need for experimenting with more selective parameter sharing.

Compared to the Danish ones, we notice that the Greek systems yield smaller but still significant improvements over the baseline, even if (a) Greek and Swedish are only distantly related and have therefore less common structures (b) the impact of untranslated OOV words is higher in Greek because of the change of alphabet: indeed, it is quite unlikely to find identical word forms in Swedish and Greek. The Greek systems have also been trained on slightly smaller bitexts (1.2M pairs, compared to 1.9M for English-Danish), but this ratio corresponds to a loss of at most 1 AER point in standard learning, which remains negligible in comparison to the cost of choosing Greek over Danish. All in all, using Greek as a bridge language is comparable to training with 10,000 English-Swedish pairs, instead of 400,000 when using Danish. This suggests that our methods can be useful even for unrelated languages in the BRIDGE scenario, even though the return ratio is much lesser than when languages are related: for Greek, 1.2M parallel sentences used cross-linguistically yield the same accuracy as 10,000 parallel sentences of the targeted pair (a ratio of approximately 1%); for Danish the ratio is closer to 20% (1.9M sentences providing the same information as 400,000 en:sv sentence pairs).

Finally, the comparison of the TR-DA and DA-TR columns shows that English-Swedish alignment biased by the English-Danish alignment is more accurate when performed in the Danish domain than in the Swedish one. Intuitively, the noisy application of a valid model performs better than a valid application of a noisy model. Columns PARAM-DA and

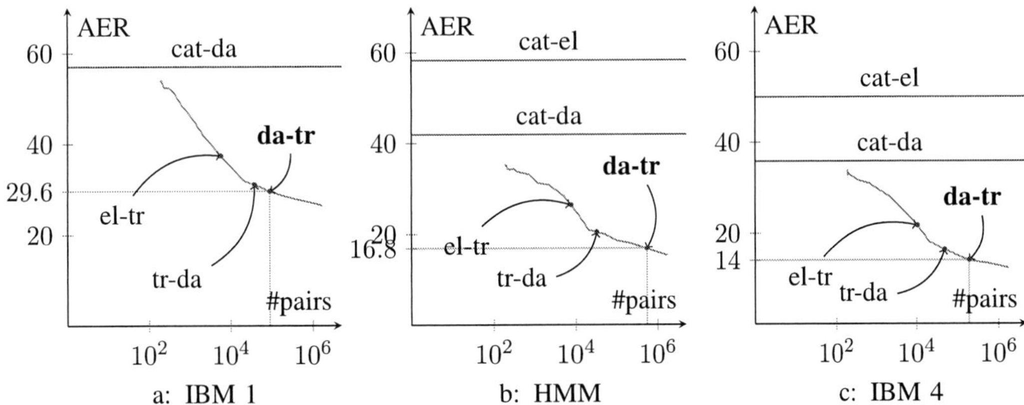

Figure 1: AER on the English-Swedish test set for increasing data sizes (red curve) and some cross-lingual methods (reported in blue along the curve). The number of English-Swedish sentence pairs includes the 192 test pairs.

	Swedish only		Danish data			Greek data			Danish parameters		
	baseline	cat-sv	cat-da	tr-da	da-tr	cat-el	tr-el	el-tr	da	glosses-da	param-da
IBM 1	53.9	**26.5**	57.0	31.1	**29.6**	74.3	**35.9**	37.4	65.94	**28.3**	33.29
HMM	35.3	**15.3**	41.9	20.5	**16.8**	58.3	26.9	**26.4**	46.74	**16.4**	25.79
IBM 4	33.9	**12.3**	35.8	16.4	**14.0**	50.0	**20.6**	21.7	49.08	**14.8**	24.34

Table 2: AER achieved by the proposed cross-lingual methods with Danish and Greek as bridge languages, compared to the baseline (unsupervised alignment on test data only) and the cat-sv higher bound (addition of large English-Swedish data).

	Swedish only		Danish data			Greek data			Danish parameters		
	baseline	cat-sv	cat-da	tr-da	da-tr	cat-el	tr-el	el-tr	da	glosses-da	param-da
IBM 1	68.7	**73.3**	58.7	73.8	**74.0**	47.4	**71.9**	71.5	66.97	**72.20**	71.07
HMM	69.9	**73.8**	71.9	73.5	**73.6**	66.6	**73.4**	71.9	69.54	**73.42**	72.43
IBM 4	73.0	**74.7**	74.0	73.9	**74.9**	72.0	73.4	**73.5**	66.67	**73.56**	71.96

Table 3: Extrinsic cross-lingual PoS accuracies achieved by the proposed cross-lingual methods with Danish and Greek as bridge languages, compared to the baseline (unsupervised alignment on test data only) and the cat-sv higher bound (addition of large English-Swedish data).

GLOSSES-DA also support that interpretation, and the fact that among the evaluated strategies, the most refined data transfer models outperform the parameter ones shows that even from a very small piece of target data, it is still possible to extract valuable knowledge to guide model adaptation to a new language.

6 Conclusion

In this work, we have presented a brief typology of general cross-lingual transfer methods and have shown how it can apply on a poorly addressed task, the transfer of bilingual knowledge. We present a few realistic scenarios where transfer of word alignment is needed and focus on one of them in the frame of unsupervised word alignment, to propose six cross-lingual methods that are easy to set up.

Experiments on an English-Swedish test set reveal that even straightforward methods can extract valuable information for weak supervision: from five sentence pairs in the bridge language, they are able to extract knowledge equivalent to one English-Swedish pair. Altogether we achieve up to 59% relative error reduction. Further analyses also provide precious hints for accurate designs of alignment transfer methods.

In future work, we intend to further explore the benefits of language similarity in the RELATED, DIRECTED BRIDGE and DIALECT scenarios, along two tracks: weighting based on linguistic similarity during the EM training and selective transfer at the sub-model level.

Acknowledgments

This work has been partly funded by the French *Direction générale de l'armement*. We thank the anonymous reviewers for their detailed comments on the paper.

References

Taylor Berg-Kirkpatrick and Dan Klein. 2010. Phylogenetic Grammar Induction. In *The 48th Annual Meeting of the Association for Computational Linguistics*, pages 1288–1297, Uppsala, Sweden.

Taylor Berg-Kirkpatrick, Alexandre Bouchard-Côté, John DeNero, and Dan Klein. 2010. Painless unsupervised learning with features. In *Human Language Technologies: The 2010 Annual Conference of the North American Chapter of the Association for Computational Linguistics*, pages 582–590.

John Blitzer. 2008. *Domain Adaptation of Natural Language Processing Systems*. Ph.D. thesis, University of Pennsylvania.

Peter F. Brown, Vincent J. Della Pietra, Stephen A. Della Pietra, and Robert L. Mercer. 1993. The mathematics of statistical machine translation: Parameter estimation. *Computational linguistics*, pages 263–311.

David Burkett, Slav Petrov, John Blitzer, and Dan Klein. 2010. Learning Better Monolingual Models with Unannotated Bilingual Text. In *Proceedings of the Fourteenth Conference on Computational Natural Language Learning*, CoNLL '10, pages 46–54.

Shay Cohen and Noah A. Smith. 2009. Shared Logistic Normal Distributions for Soft Parameter Tying in Unsupervised Grammar Induction. In *Proceedings of Human Language Technologies: The 2009 Annual Conference of the North American Chapter of the Association for Computational Linguistics*, pages 74–82, Boulder, Colorado.

Shay B. Cohen, Dipanjan Das, and Noah A. Smith. 2011. Unsupervised Structure Prediction with Non-Parallel Multilingual Guidance. In *Proceedings of the 2011 Conference on Empirical Methods in Natural Language Processing*, pages 50–61, Edinburgh, Scotland, UK., July.

Dipanjan Das and Slav Petrov. 2011. Unsupervised Part-of-speech Tagging with Bilingual Graph-based Projections. In *Proceedings of the 49th Annual Meeting of the Association for Computational Linguistics: Human Language Technologies - Volume 1*, HLT '11, pages 600–609.

Chris Dyer, Victor Chahuneau, and Noah A. Smith. 2013. A Simple, Fast, and Effective Reparameterization of IBM Model 2. In *Proceedings of NAACL 2013, the Conference of the North American Chapter of the Association for Computational Linguistics: Human Language Technologies*, pages 644–648, Atlanta, Georgia.

Maud Ehrmann, Marco Turchi, and Ralf Steinberger. 2011. Building a Multilingual Named Entity-Annotated Corpus Using Annotation Projection. In *Proceedings of the International Conference Recent Advances in Natural Language Processing*, pages 118–124, Hissar, Bulgaria.

Alexander Fraser and Daniel Marcu. 2007. Measuring word alignment quality for statistical machine translation. *Computational Linguistics*, pages 293–303.

Kuzman Ganchev, Jennifer Gillenwater, and Ben Taskar. 2009. Dependency Grammar Induction via Bitext Projection Constraints. In *Proceedings of the Joint Conference of the 47th Annual Meeting of the ACL and the 4th International Joint Conference on Natural Language Processing of the AFNLP: Volume 1 - Volume 1*, ACL '09, pages 369–377.

Stephan Gouws, Yoshua Bengio, and Greg Corrado. 2015. BilBOWA: Fast Bilingual Distributed Representations without Word Alignments. In David Blei and Francis Bach, editors, *Proceedings of the 32nd International Conference on Machine Learning*, pages 748–756. JMLR Workshop and Conference Proceedings.

Jiri Hana, Anna Feldman, and Chris Brew. 2004. A Resource-light Approach to Russian Morphology: Tagging Russian using Czech resources. In Dekang Lin and Dekai Wu, editors, *Proceedings of EMNLP 2004*, pages 222–229, Barcelona, Spain, July.

Maria Holmqvist and Lars Ahrenberg. 2011. A Gold Standard for English–Swedish Word Alignment. In *Proceedings of the 18th Nordic Conference of Computational Linguistics NODALIDA*, pages 106–113.

Wu Hua, Wang Haifeng, and Liu Zhanyi. 2005. Alignment model adaptation for domain-specific word alignment. In *Proceedings of the 43rd Annual Meeting on Association for Computational Linguistics*, pages 467–474.

Rebecca Hwa, Philip Resnik, A.Weinberg, C. Cabezas, and O. Kolak. 2005. Bootstrapping Parsers via Syntactic Projection across Parallel Texts. *Natural language engineering*, 11:311–325.

Jagadeesh Jagarlamudi, Raghavendra Udupa, Hal Daume III, and Abhijit Bhole. 2011. Improving Bilingual Projections via Sparse Covariance Matrices. In *Proceedings of the 2011 Conference on Empirical Methods in Natural Language Processing*, pages 930–940, Edinburgh, Scotland, UK.

Philipp Koehn. Europarl: A Parallel Corpus for Statistical Machine Translation, year = 2005. In *2nd Workshop on EBMT of MT-Summit X*, pages 79–86, Phuket, Thailand.

Tomáš Kočiský, Karl Moritz Hermann, and Phil Blunsom. 2014. Learning Bilingual Word Representations by Marginalizing Alignments. In *Proceedings of the 52nd Annual Meeting of the Association for Computational Linguistics (Volume 2: Short Papers)*, pages 224–229, Baltimore, Maryland, June.

Mikhail Kozhevnikov and Ivan Titov. 2013. Bootstrapping Semantic Role Labelers from Parallel Data. In *Second Joint Conference on Lexical and Computational Semantics (*SEM), Volume 1: Proceedings of the Main Conference and the Shared Task: Semantic Textual Similarity*, pages 317–327, Atlanta, Georgia, USA.

Shankar Kumar, Franz Josef Och, and Wolfgang Macherey. 2007. Improving Word Alignment with Bridge Languages. In *EMNLP-CoNLL*, pages 42–50.

Ophélie Lacroix, Lauriane Aufrant, Guillaume Wisniewski, and François Yvon. 2016a. Frustratingly Easy Cross-Lingual Transfer for Transition-Based Dependency Parsing. In *The 15th Annual Conference of the North American Chapter of the Association for Computational Linguistics: Human Language Technologies*, NAACL 2016, San Diego, California, USA.

Ophélie Lacroix, Guillaume Wisnewski, and François Yvon. 2016b. Cross-lingual Dependency Transfer: What Matters? Assessing the Impact of Pre- and Postprocessing. In *Proceedings of the NAACL-16 Workshop on Multilingual and Crosslingual Methods in NLP*, MLCL 2016, San Diego, CA, USA. Association for Computational Linguistics.

Patrik Lambert, Yanjun Ma, Sylwia Ozdowska, and Andy Way. 2009. Tracking relevant alignment characteristics for machine translation. In *Proceedings of Machine Translation Summit XII*, pages 268–275.

Patrik Lambert, Simon Petitrenaud, Yanjun Ma, and Andy Way. 2010. Statistical analysis of alignment characteristics for phrase-based machine translation. In *Proceedings of the 14th European Association for Machine Translation*.

Tomer Levinboim and David Chiang. 2015. Multi-Task Word Alignment Triangulation for Low-Resource Languages. In *Proceedings of the 2015 Conference of the North American Chapter of the Association for Computational Linguistics: Human Language Technologies*, pages 1221–1226.

Zhenghua Li, Min Zhang, and Wenliang Chen. 2014. Soft Cross-lingual Syntax Projection for Dependency Parsing. In *Proceedings of COLING 2014, the 25th International Conference on Computational Linguistics: Technical Papers*, pages 783–793, Dublin, Ireland. Dublin City University and Association for Computational Linguistics.

Adam Lopez and Philip Resnik. 2006. Word-Based Alignment, Phrase-Based Translation: What's the Link? In *Proceedings of AMTA*, pages 90–99.

Ryan McDonald, Slav Petrov, and Keith Hall. 2011. Multi-source Transfer of Delexicalized Dependency Parsers. In *Proceedings of EMNLP 2011, the Conference on Empirical Methods in Natural Language Processing*, pages 62–72.

Ryan McDonald, Joakim Nivre, Yvonne Quirmbach-Brundage, Yoav Goldberg, Dipanjan Das, Kuzman Ganchev, Keith Hall, Slav Petrov, Hao Zhang, Oscar Täckström, Claudia Bedini, Núria Bertomeu Castelló, and Jungmee Lee. 2013. Universal Dependency Annotation for Multilingual Parsing. In *Proceedings of the 51st Annual Meeting of the Association for Computational Linguistics (Volume 2: Short Papers)*, pages 92–97, Sofia, Bulgaria, August.

Robert C. Moore. 2005. A discriminative framework for bilingual word alignment. In *Proceedings of the conference on Human Language Technology and Empirical Methods in Natural Language Processing*, pages 81–88.

Franz Josef Och and Hermann Ney. 2000. A comparison of alignment models for statistical machine translation. In *Proceedings of the 18th conference on Computational linguistics-Volume 2*, pages 1086–1090.

Franz Josef Och and Hermann Ney. 2003. A systematic comparison of various statistical alignment models. *Computational linguistics*, pages 19–51.

Oscar Täckström, Ryan McDonald, and Jakob Uszkoreit. 2012. Cross-lingual Word Clusters for Direct Transfer of Linguistic Structure. In *Proceedings of the 2012 Conference of the North American Chapter of the Association for Computational Linguistics: Human Language Technologies*, NAACL HLT '12, pages 477–487, Stroudsburg, PA, USA.

Oscar Täckström, Dipanjan Das, Slav Petrov, Ryan McDonald, and Joakim Nivre. 2013. Token and Type Constraints for Cross-Lingual Part-of-Speech Tagging. *Transactions of the Association for Computational Linguistics*, 1:1–12.

Jörg Tiedemann. 2014. Rediscovering Annotation Projection for Cross-Lingual Parser Induction. In *Proceedings of the 25th International Conference on Computational Linguistics (COLING): Technical Papers*, pages 1854–1864, Dublin, Ireland.

Stephan Vogel, Hermann Ney, and Christoph Tillmann. 1996. HMM-Based Word Alignment in Statistical Translation. In *Proceedings of the 16th conference on Computational linguistics-Volume 2*, pages 836–841.

Mengqiu Wang and Christopher D. Manning. 2014. Cross-lingual Projected Expectation Regularization for Weakly Supervised Learning. *Transactions of the ACL*, 2(1):55–66.

Haifeng Wang, Hua Wu, and Zhanyi Liu. 2006. Word alignment for languages with scarce resources using bilingual corpora of other language pairs. In *Proceedings of the COLING/ACL on Main conference poster sessions*, pages 874–881.

Guillaume Wisniewski, Nicolas Pécheux, Souhir Gahbiche-Braham, and François Yvon. 2014. Cross-Lingual Part-of-Speech Tagging through Ambiguous Learning. In *Proceedings of the 2014 Conference on Empirical Methods in Natural Language Processing*, pages 1779–1785.

David Yarowsky, Grace Ngai, and Richard Wicentowski. 2001. Inducing Multilingual Text Analysis Tools via Robust Projection Across Aligned Corpora. In *Proceedings of the First International Conference on Human Language Technology Research*, HLT '01, pages 1–8.

Daniel Zeman and Philip Resnik. 2008. Cross-Language Parser Adaptation between Related Languages. In *Proceedings of the IJCNLP-08 Workshop on NLP for Less Privileged Languages*, pages 35–42, Hyderabad, India, January. Asian Federation of Natural Language Processing.

Leveraging Data-Driven Methods in Word-Level Language Identification for a Multilingual Alpine Heritage Corpus

Ada Wan
University of Zurich
`ada.wan@uzh.ch`

Abstract

This paper presents a data-driven, simple cluster-and-label approach using optimized count-based methods for word-level language identification for a large domain-specific multilingual diachronic corpus of periodicals published at least yearly between 1864 and 2014 in Switzerland. Our system requires no annotated data or training, only minimal human effort in evaluating and labeling 50 clusters for a corpus of almost 40 million tokens. Despite being unsupervised, our results show an accuracy that is comparable to the corpus annotations which result from an existing code switching algorithm and the combined usage of two supervised systems using character and byte n-gram models (Volk and Clematide, 2014).

1 Introduction

Language identification (LID) is important in NLP so long as the applications and tools designed and used are language-specific. Many tokenizers, POS-taggers, lemmatization and NER systems suffer in performance when met with sporadic sequences of foreign/unknown elements – this is especially the case when the languages in question are lesser known, the domain is more specific, and/or the training material is scarce. The view that LID is a "solved task" is unfortunately a misconception that is based on the success of work that dealt with document-level LID in a small number of languages (Lui, 2014). Real world data, esp. those with much code switching (CS), the phenomenon that occurs when speakers/writers switch back and forth between at

least two languages in communication, on smaller spans of texts or with mixed genres, continue to pose challenges.

In this paper, we present our initial LID effort for a large, domain-specific, yet very diverse in themes and styles, multilingual diachronic corpus of periodicals published by the *Swiss Alpine Club* (SAC) abound with intrasentential CS instances. CS in this corpus has previously been addressed in Volk and Clematide (2014) who use a set of heuristics to identify code-switching candidates and label these using *langid.py*[1] (Lui and Baldwin, 2012), an off-the-shelf Python package providing a supervised multinomial Naive Bayes classifier that has been trained over a mixture of byte n-grams ($1 \leq n \leq 4$) on 97 languages. In contrast, we attempt to tackle this task through a simple cluster-and-label approach with unsupervised word vectors. Our system – requiring only minimal human intervention when labeling the induced clusters – achieves comparable performance to the existing CS annotations, demonstrating the feasibility of unsupervised word clustering for LID for our corpus.

2 Related Work

Word-level language identification has been tackled mostly through supervised approaches in prior work. For example, King and Abney (2013) show that the problem can be framed as a sequence labeling problem and that hidden Markov Model (HMM) and Conditional Random Fields (CRFs) can be trained – starting from monolingual data – to perform reasonably well at labeling words in multilingual texts.

---

[1] `https://pypi.python.org/pypi/langid`

45

Proceedings of the Workshop on Multilingual and Cross-lingual Methods in NLP, pages 45–54,
San Diego, California, June 17, 2016. ©2016 Association for Computational Linguistics

In the first shared task on LID on code-switched data from 2014, system architectures ranged from a rule-based system to ones leveraging word embeddings, extended Markov Models, and CRF autoencoders (Solorio et al., 2014). While most teams focused on multilingual LID systems for the shared task, there are approaches that deal with classification on bilingual code-switched texts specifically – for example, Jhamtani et al. (2014) build a system that makes use of several heuristic features, including a special edit distance between Hindi and English that fits their use case for "Hinglish" texts.

On the other hand, unsupervised approaches to word-level language identification have not been as popular. A cluster-and-label approach similar to ours has recently been applied to unsupervised "Translationese" detection for machine translation by Rabinovich and Wintner (2015), but only for text passages of 2000 tokens each. Another characteristic that sets apart their approach from ours is the cluster labeling approach. Their automatic labeling approach builds "representative" language models for the class labels and then assigns them to the unsupervised clusters by comparing them to the empirical distributions in the clusters. Since their approach is not applicable in our case and labeling clusters for our task requires rather little effort, we resorted to manual labeling.

3 Data: SAC Yearbooks from Text+Berg (TB)

Text+Berg digital[2] is an ongoing text digitization and annotation project for alpine texts. The yearbooks published by the SAC form a substantial part of the corpus. They contain "reports and essays on all aspects of alpinism as well as alpine nature and culture" and cover a good range of sub-genres: from more literary essays and anecdotal narratives on mountain expeditions, book reviews and poems, to practical travel tips such as hotel reviews and cabin directories, to more scientific studies of living organisms, glacier and climate observations, geo-historical descriptions on cols, mountains, and parks, and on the flora and fauna of the Alps and other mountain regions, to more technical accident and security reports and financial reports from protocols of the annual club gatherings (Volk and Clematide, 2014).

From the first edition of the yearbook in 1864 to 1923, the publication appeared yearly under the title *Jahrbuch des SAC*, and from 1925 until present, *Die Alpen. Les Alpes. Le Alpi.* Although it has been published monthly since 1996, the issues have been archived yearly as the yearbooks therebefore by TB – one XML file per year, and are referred to here as the yearbooks. Before 1957, these yearbooks are written without translation in mixed languages – German, French, Italian, and Romansch (as far as we know). That is, an article or a sentence in one language may contain passages or word(s) in one or many other language(s) without translation. Since 1957 there have been parallel versions of these yearbooks in German and in French, with the addition of Italian since 2012. But despite the emergence of these parallel versions, the occurrences of CS remains rather consistent throughout the years. Each of these parallel versions is archived as one XML file per year. For these 150 years between 1864 and 2014, there are 209 XML files (there was no publication in years 1870, 1915, and 1924), with roughly 39 million tokens in total after conversion into plain text, which we used as data for our study. The yearbooks from 1864 to 2000 were scanned and converted into text with commercial OCR software by *TB digital*. Through a crowdsourcing initiative, selected yearbooks have been manually inspected and almost all OCR errors from these books were corrected. The texts from 2001 to 2009 were extracted from PDFs. From 2010 on, *TB digital* has been directly receiving the publication in XML format from the SAC and converting these into the XML files with linguistic annotations available for download for research purposes.

Up to and including the latest release of the yearbooks (release 151v01, from April 11, 2015), all TB corpora have been LIDed on the sentence-level for all sentences with more than 40 characters using *Lingua-Ident*[3] by Michael Piotrowski, a statistical language identifier based on character n-gram frequencies. (Results for shorter sentences and for Romansch (RM) were found to be unreliable and

---

[2] http://textberg.ch

[3] http://search.cpan.org/dist/Lingua-Ident

these were hence assigned language tag of the previous sentence or that of the article). *Lingua-Ident* is able to recognize sentences in German (DE), French (FR), Italian (IT), and English (EN) thus far. Swiss-German (CH-DE) requires additional processing. While it is safe to narrow the number of dominant languages of the corpus down to 6 – the four official languages of Switzerland (DE, FR, IT, RM), in addition to EN and CH-DE – automatically determining exhaustively what other languages it contains will remain a hard problem. In our manual evaluation phase for the present experiment, we notice Latin (LA) and Spanish (ES) elements in the corpus, which confirm the observation by Volk and Clematide (2014), but we also found texts in Danish (DA) and Tibetan (BO) (in Roman script), for instance. As described in the following section, we approach our LID task as a closed-class classification problem (with 8 classes/labels) after clustering our word vectors.

4   Method

We adopt an unsupervised data-driven approach in clustering word vectors, optimized with lessons learned from Levy et al. (2015) by combining a PPMI (positive pointwise mutual information) matrix with a constant-sized weighted context window, after extracting plain text from each of the XML files for the SAC yearbooks. Our goal is to assign a label (i.e. a language class) to each word type in our data.

4.1   Word Vector Representation: PPMI matrix with weighted context window

We take as vocabulary V all word types v that neither are punctuations nor numbers, nor do they contain any. That is, tokens such as *1er* were excluded, regardless of whether it could be a permissible sequence in a language or an OCR error. We take as context words all elements of V that occur at least 100 times (for reasons of scalability), and refer to the set of these context words as C. We represent our data by constructing a high dimensional $|V| \times |C|$ matrix M with one row for each word type v and with one column for each context word c. This results in a 785,266 x 23,263 matrix.

We collect co-occurrence counts for every pair (v, c) using a context window of 5. Concretely,

we treat each yearbook file as a sequence of tokens, $w_1, \ldots, w_N$, where N is the total number of these "eligible" (non-punctuation, non-numeric) tokens. For each w_i such that $w_i \in V$, we give a weighted count to each of the surrounding words, provided that they are in C: $\frac{1}{5}$ for w_{i-5} and w_{i+5}, $\frac{2}{5}$ for w_{i-4} and w_{i+4}, $\frac{3}{5}$ for w_{i-3} and w_{i+3}, $\frac{4}{5}$ for w_{i-2} and w_{i+2}, and 1 (i.e. $\frac{5}{5}$) for w_{i-1} and w_{i+1}. (Note that the context window is fixed, e.g. if only one of the surrounding words is in C, or if there is only one surrounding word, only one count will be collected, the window does not expand in order to collect counts 5 times.) We sum up these counts from all yearbooks.

The value of each matrix cell M_{jk} is the weighted co-occurrence count of (v_j, c_k) transformed into a normalized association measure, PPMI, where

$$PPMI(v, c) = \max(PMI(v, c), 0) \qquad (1)$$

$$PMI(v, c) = \frac{\log P(v, c)}{P(v)P(c)} \qquad (2)$$

and $P(v, c)$, $P(v)$, and $P(c)$ are estimated using maximum likelihood from the co-occurrence counts.

Pointwise mutual information (PMI), defined in eq. 2, is an association metric for measuring word association norms based on the information theoretic concept of mutual information. PMI compares the joint probability of two events with the product of their marginal probabilities.

Proposed by Church and Hanks (1990), the PMI of two events x, y is interpreted as follows:

> $PMI(x, y) \gg 0$ means that there is a genuine association between x and y, as P(x,y) will be much larger than P(x)P(y)
>
> $PMI(x, y) \approx 0$ implies that there is no interesting relationship between x and y, as P(x,y) $\approx$ P(x)P(y)
>
> $PMI(x, y) \ll 0$ means that x and y are in complementary distribution, as P(x,y) will be much less than P(x)P(y).

Since there could be many entries in the PPMI matrix where (x, y) were never observed in the data, yielding $-\infty$ as $PMI(x,y) = \log 0$, we adopt the common practical solution of using PPMI, in which all negative PMI values are replaced by 0 (see eq. 1).

4.2 Dimensionality Reduction: Truncated Singular Value Decomposition (TSVD)

SVD factorizes a matrix M into the product of three matrices $U \cdot \Sigma \cdot V^T$, where U and V are orthonormal and Σ is a diagonal matrix of eigenvalues in decreasing order. When this factorized matrix is truncated, only the largest/top d diagonal elements of Σ are "kept". In other words, TSVD compresses the major associative patterns in the data into a lower dimensional matrix by ignoring the smaller, less important influences (Deerwester et al., 1990).

As mentioned in Section 4.1, our PPMI matrix has 23,263 columns, and despite its sparsity, the original word vector file is 37 GB in size. To facilitate our clustering experiments in the subsequent step, we reduce the dimensions of these word vectors to 100 using TSVD[4], resulting in a new file size of 1.21 GB (a reduction of nearly 97%).

4.3 Clustering: K-means

TSVD only gives us a matrix of reduced dimensions. But the number of words we have to cluster is still fairly high (785,266). K-means, as a flat, as opposed to hierarchical, clustering algorithm, is an efficient solution for our task. The objective of K-means is to minimize the average squared Euclidean distance of word vectors from their cluster centers where a cluster center is defined as the mean or centroid $\vec{\mu}$ of the word vectors in a cluster ω (Manning et al., 2008):

$$\vec{\mu}(\omega) = \frac{1}{|\omega|} \sum_{\vec{v} \in \omega} \vec{v} \qquad (3)$$

K in *K-means* refers to the number of clusters prespecified by the user. To obtain 50 clusters from our data, we first initialize 50 points (i.e. means) to random values, seeding the random generator with a random seed. The algorithm comprises two steps: the assignment step, in which each data point is assigned to the nearest centroid, giving rise to 50 clusters with one centroid for each cluster, and the update step, in which the centroids are then adjusted

such that they represent the mean values of all the data points in the clusters formed in the assignment step. This is repeated until the cluster assignments converge.

In order to find a set of clusters that is most representative of our data, we run several clustering experiments varying the number of clusters. Ideally, we would get vocabulary items of a language to cluster together such that we get one cluster per language. As may be expected, the situation is a bit more complicated – e.g. if we divide up our data into 5 clusters, we get 1 mixed, 1 IT and 1 FR cluster, and 2 DE clusters. This tendency remains rather stable irrespective of the clustering algorithm used. In contrast, the number of clusters considerably impacts cluster quality. If too few clusters are used, only the strongest tendency of the data can be captured and minority languages such as RM and EN would be lumped together with the majority languages DE/FR/IT or contribute to mixed clusters. As we increase the number of clusters, purer clusters emerge and mixed classes become smaller. However, beyond a certain point, these improvements seem to level off – 100 clusters are not necessarily purer than 50 clusters. In earlier experiments, we compared both the scikit-learn implementation of a non-parametric Dirichlet Process Gaussian Mixture Model (DPGMM) which automatically determines the appropriate number of clusters from the data[5] and a parametric approach using K-means with 50 clusters. The non-parametric model found, depending on the choice of a spherical, diagonal, or full covariance matrix, 194, 201, and 4 clusters respectively. While we knew that 4 clusters would be too few, we measured performance of the other two against K-means (see Table 1) and decided to go with K-means for clustering as more clusters do not necessarily entail purer clusters or better results.

We found a set of 50 clusters (which are formed using the vectors we have been describing – these vectors differ from those in earlier experiments only in some minor variation in symbols filtered out in the process of vector building) we produced using K-means yields fairly reasonable language group-

---

[4]via the implementation in scikit-learn (Pedregosa et al., 2011): `http://scikit-learn.org/stable/modules/generated/sklearn.decomposition.TruncatedSVD.html`

[5]One still has to provide an upper bound on the number of clusters for inference using scikit-learn. We chose 1,000.

	tsvd_dpgmm_diag (201 clusters)	tsvd_dpgmm_spherical (194 clusters)	tsvd_kmeans (50 clusters)
strict	88.78	88.60	88.88
lenient	89.39	89.30	89.55

Table 1: Accuracy scores (rounded to 2 digits) from non-parametric (Dirichlet Process Gaussian Mixture Model) vs. parametric models (K-means), using vectors built in earlier experiments

ings, as even minority languages such as RM and EN could be represented as classes of their own. We hence use it for evaluation of our TBLID system in this paper.

4.4 Evaluating and Labeling of Clusters

We evaluate the clusters manually and assign labels (language classes) in a majority rule fashion. If the first 20 most frequent words in a cluster look to be from one language, that language is assigned as one of the class labels: DE, EN, FR, IT, RM, CH-DE, NE (named entity), or MIXED (if words are not in any of the aforementioned classes). (See Figure 1 for examples of clusters that were labeled DE, FR, IT, EN, and RM.) Most of the time, there is a majority class in a cluster. In cases where it was difficult to make a call based on the top 20 words, the remainder of the cluster will be looked at and evaluated.

The need for a separate class for NEs is based on cluster results[6]. Although certain NEs have variants in different languages, e.g. the Swiss city of Basel is *Basel* in DE, *Bâle* in FR, *Basilea* in IT, and these words could fall into their respective language classes, results of various clustering experiments show that, especially when the number of classes are well above the number of language classes, some NEs do tend to cluster together.

5 Evaluation of TBLID and Results

5.1 Evaluation Setup

With one language class label assigned for each vocabulary item, our experiment to evaluate our LID system (henceforth: TBLID) begins by randomly selecting sentences that are indicated to contain CS segments based on the annotations that are about

___
[6]but this also concurs with the annotation guidelines for the shared task in EMNLP 2014 Workshop on Computational Approaches to Code Switching: `http://emnlp2014.org/workshops/ CodeSwitch/guideline/word_annotations _en_es_CF.pdf`

to be included in the upcoming release of the yearbooks provided by *TB digital*. These annotations result from the implementation of the CS detection algorithm from Volk and Clematide (2014) (hereafter: VCCS) which uses a combination of four factors (the presence of quotation marks, at least 2 tokens being outside of these quotation marks, lemma tags ⟨unknown⟩, and minimum CS segment length of 15 characters) as cues to identify CS instances. According to these criteria, 194 of the 209 yearbook files contain at least one CS sentence. We randomly select one CS sentence from each of these 194 files to evaluate TBLID based on word-level language label accuracy and to compare our labels to the TB annotations which are output of *langid.py* for the intra-sentential CS segments and *Lingua-Ident* on the sentence level. (Classifying words one by one using *langid.py* alone for these 194 sentences yielded an overall accuracy of approximately 36%, hence it will not be used for comparison in this study.)

Word-level language identification accuracy is the percentage of the correctly labeled word tokens (i.e. tokens containing no numeric element or punctuation except for hyphen(s), apostrophe(s), and period(s)) from all sentences with CS. 2 of these 194 sentences are disqualified for evaluation due to indecipherability as they consist exclusively of numeric elements and abbreviations, most of which are potential OCR errors. This leaves us with a total of 5,073 word tokens.

We illustrate scoring here with the following sentence from the 1925 yearbook:

> [1] Je n' en sais rien , mais l' énergie de son «
> Oel per oel e daint per daint » résonne encore
> à mon oreille .

The 22 word tokens here should be identified with the following languages (labels indicated here with preceding underscores, CS segment boldfaced):

> [1a] **GOLD**: Je_fr n'_fr en_fr sais_fr rien_fr
> , mais_fr l'_fr énergie_fr de_fr son_fr «

14	uhr	25266	4	camp	7118	5	cima	3157	45	alps	645	41	sv	197
14	nacht	7296	4	mal	6198	5	passo	2373	45	mountains	597	41	lub	180
14	stunde	7217	4	hôtel	2769	5	vi	1906	45	lake	593	41	zei	102
14	sonne	7183	4	halte	1904	5	lago	1848	45	range	445	41	isa	97
14	morgen	6240	4	étions	1704	5	punta	1780	45	himalayan	399	41	lps	90
14	himmel	5676	4	chaud	1594	5	circa	1721	45	black	389	41	ais	89
14	nebel	5491	4	chance	1559	5	dalle	1668	45	karakoram	388	41	pü	84
14	lager	3598	4	tentative	1527	5	campo	1547	45	for	364	41	lur	75
14	verlassen	3208	4	trouvé	1515	5	rifugio	1491	45	mountaineering	360	41	dais	75
14	licht	2962	4	arrivée	1509	5	io	1424	45	moore	351	41	sün	74
14	wolken	2623	4	après-midi	1481	5	alpino	1070	45	no.	339	41	aint	73
14	morgens	2586	4	arriver	1412	5	gran	1003	45	sikkim	326	41	scu	70
14	rast	2577	4	perdu	1394	5	termine	905	45	garhwal	316	41	svizzer	63
14	stein	2512	4	compagnie	1258	5	ti	812	45	valley	308	41	izz	61
14	hotel	2454	4	attendre	1235	5	pur	789	45	ice	304	41	naiv	59
14	früh	2416	4	gravi	1219	5	pure	778	45	kenya	291	41	tuot	52
14	abends	2380	4	tempête	1210	5	no	736	45	snow	290	41	suot	52
14	kopf	2350	4	étape	1172	5	bel	686	45	douglas	289	41	eira	49
14	rucksack	2172	4	réussi	1149	5	né	664	45	ladakh	280	41	daint	47
14	halb	2091	4	souvenir	1130	5	porta	661	45	hudson	280	41	sco	46

Figure 1: Examples of clusters labeled DE, FR, IT, EN, and RM (from left to right). The leftmost column of the three columns for each language (i.e. inside each frame) indicates the cluster number, the middle column the word token, the rightmost the term frequency.

Oel_rm per_rm oel_rm e_rm daint_rm per_rm daint_rm » résonne_fr encore_fr à_fr mon_fr oreille_fr .

Annotations by *TB digital* (punctuation marks are also classified by their system, but excluded from evaluation for this paper) have 15 of these correctly identified as FR and 7 RM words incorrectly identified as OC (Occitan):

[1b] **TB (Lingua-Ident + langid):** Je_fr n'_fr en_fr sais_fr rien_fr ,_fr mais_fr l'_fr énergie_fr de_fr son_fr «_oc **Oel_oc per_oc oel_oc e_oc daint_oc per_oc daint_oc** »_oc résonne_fr encore_fr à_fr mon_fr oreille_fr ._fr

TBLID has 17 correctly identified word tokens and makes 5 mistakes (non-word tokens were excluded as mentioned, and given _*unk* tags):

[1c] **TBLID:** Je_fr n'_fr en_fr sais_fr rien_fr ,_unk mais_fr l'_fr énergie_fr de_fr son_fr «_unk **Oel_mixed per_it oel_mixed e_it daint_rm per_it daint_rm** »_unk résonne_fr encore_fr à_fr mon_fr oreille_fr ._unk

If *oel* were a word in a language not available in the set of language classes in TBLID, classifying it as MIXED would be acceptable and expected, but since RM is a possible label, each occurrence of *oel*, for example, is counted as 1 incorrect instance.

All word tokens are evaluated in context, in the particular instance, not for their potentiality to take on a certain label. E.g. the two word tokens *par an* meaning *yearly* in a FR segment should both be labeled FR, even though *par* can be DE/EN/FR/IT/RM, and *an* can be an EN, FR, DE, as well as a RM word, if evaluated independently. We will return to the issue of multilingual homographs in our discussion in Section 6.1 below.

5.2 NE Classification and Two Annotation Schemes

On the one hand, it can be non-trivial to pinpoint what kinds of NEs the clusters are supposed to classify when it is more so the case that certain "proper-noun-looking" nouns tend to form their own clusters; on the other hand, we do see cases that make "human sense", such as names of months of a language clustering together. For the purpose of this

LID task, we define organizations, person names, locations (which include mountain and cabin names), and month names as NEs.

Since NE is not an available category in TB annotations, we consider an NE correct if an LID system gives it an NE or a correct language label. But this notion of "correct language" can be an intricate matter with such an inherently code-switched corpus. We may understand that, for example, within a DE segment, if the word *Bâle* was used when there is a valid DE variant *Basel* available, there is valid reason to consider this as a CS element. But how about in cases where the form of the name is identical across the languages in question, such as *Bonn*? The usage of *Bonn* in midst of a FR segment may not be considered CS in that case. But the line here, if there is one, can be blurry. Consider the following sentence from the 1975 German yearbook:

> [2] Indessen gibt dann der Guide bleu von 1962 einige Details über die Bedingungen für eine Besteigung bekannt , indem er von der alten Ausgabe die Erwähnung warmer Kleidung , guter Schuhe und Schutzbrillen übernimmt , aber alles in Verbindung mit «Grand Hotel Ätna , mehreren Restaurants bei der Casa Cantoniera , Schutzhütte Sapienza , Hütte Menza des CAI , Wintersport etc . »

If annotated with the above rationale (sentence truncated to highlight only the more relevant parts):

> [2a] **GOLD-strict:** Indessen_de gibt_de dann_de der_de **Guide_de bleu_de** von_de 1962_unk einige_de Details_de über_de die_de Bedingungen_de für_de eine_de Besteigung_de bekannt_de , ... , mehreren_de Restaurants_de bei_de der_de **Casa_de_ne Cantoniera_de_ne** , Schutzhütte_ne_de **Sapienza_ne_de** , Hütte_de_ne **Menza_de_ne** des_de **CAI_ne_de** , Wintersport_de etc_de . »

Classifying *Guide bleu*, *Casa Cantoniera*, *Sapienza*, *Menza*, and *CAI* (which stands for *Club alpino Italiano*) as DE may not be uncontested, perhaps even a bit unintuitive for some. We hence devised two evaluation schemes – strict and lenient. The annotations as exemplified in [2a] are considered strict. The lenient annotations are illustrated in [2b] below:

	Lingua-Ident + langid.py	TBLID
strict	89.73	89.33
lenient	89.81	89.91

Table 2: Final accuracy scores (rounded to 2 digits), based on 5073 words

> [2b] **GOLD-lenient:** Indessen_de gibt_de dann_de der_de **Guide_de_fr bleu_de_fr** von_de 1962_unk einige_de Details_de über_de die_de Bedingungen_de für_de eine_de Besteigung_de bekannt_de , ... , mehreren_de Restaurants_de bei_de der_de **Casa_de_ne_it Cantoniera_de_ne_it** , Schutzhütte_ne_de **Sapienza_ne_de_it** , Hütte_de_ne **Menza_de_ne_it** des_de **CAI_ne_de_it** , Wintersport_de etc_de . »

There can be more than one permissible language for each word. For the word *Casa* here, for example, a label is considered correct if it is DE, NE, or IT. The strict annotations for a word are a subset of the lenient annotations.

5.3 Results

Despite being a very weakly supervised system (manual "supervision" took place only in the labeling of 50 clusters), the combination of the two fully supervised systems and TBLID performed neck and neck. As expected, the strict annotation standard favors the combination of *Lingua-Ident* and *langid.py*, which assumes the notion of a base language for each chunk of texts within a sentence. TBLID is word-level and allows for more flexible switching and more variation in languages within a sentence, hence agrees more with the lenient annotation standard. In the strict evaluation, TB annotations have 4552 out of 5073 word tokens correct, with an accuracy score of 89.73%, while TBLID has 4532 correct, at 89.33%. In the lenient evaluation, TBLID has 4561 correct, i.e. accuracy of 89.91%, whereas TB annotations only have 4556 correct, at 89.81% (all scores are rounded to 2 decimal places), as summarized in Table 2.

6 Error Analysis and Future Directions

6.1 Multilingual Homographs

The issue that came first to our attention was effected by what we term "multilingual homographs" (MHs) and the system of assigning one label per word.

Generally, a homograph (within one language) is a word form that expresses two or more different meanings, e.g. *bass* in EN can refer to a fish and a musical instrument. In our study, we use MH to refer to a word form that exists in two or more languages. TBLID assigns one label to each word type, that is, word type of a multilingual corpus. This immediately poses a problem, above all, to the scores of stopwords that the few Indo-European languages in this corpus have in common. Word forms such as *la, il, le, de, da, des, d', an, in, on, per, si, non, et, i, was, a, je* as well as *aller, va, est, qua, be, god[7], ni, sur, at, mal, termine* are eligible word forms in more than one of the languages relevant in our LID task. Close to about 100 instances where TBLID "mis-labeled" in this evaluation were of errors related to MHs. For example, the TBLID label for the word *des* (meaning: "of the" in FR and DE) is FR. Hence whenever *des* in DE appears, our current "one label per word type"-design suffers an inevitable defeat (and a frequent one too as *des* occurs not at all seldom in DE). We tried to remedy this situation by attempting to assign multiple labels via soft clustering with EM (Expectation Maximization) and TSVD via scikit-learn. But the distribution of these MHs are so skewed that it was difficult to even pick a threshold above which the word should be classified as belonging to a certain cluster. Most of these popular MHs, despite their multiple identities, (oddly) show a strong preference for one cluster with a probability of almost 1.

Since it is less likely for function words to be an independent CS element, modeling context through a sequential model such as HMM and CRF as in King and Abney (2013) after our clustering effort could be helpful. Instances such as the one in Section 6.2 below are good test cases for these future experiments. They serve as vivid reminders that relying on the LID of a larger stretch of text for a base language can also be prone to missing many cases of CS and correct LID.

6.2 CS Detection Heuristic: Quotation Marks

One frequent error pattern for TB annotations is the assumption of quotation marks playing a role in CS. The following sentence from the 1997 FR yearbook contains a long stretch of pairs of words in the form "FR / DE" with figures reporting the financial gains, losses, and interests of the SAC fund. The sentence was extracted as a CS candidate for evaluation due to the « and » towards the end of the sentence:

> [3] Franz Werthmüller , chef des finances … Zins / Intérêts … Material Rettungswesen / Matériel de sauvetage … Veränderung Clubvermögen / Variation de la fortune du club … Zunahme / Augmentation … Abnahme / Diminution Zu- und Abgänge FondsAttributions et débits des fonds Verzinsung der Fonds / Intérêts des fonds Zunahme Allgemeine Reserven / Augmentation Réserves générales … Details siehe Tabelle « Veränderung der Fonds » / Détails :

VCCS assumes elements outside of quotation marks to be in one (base/default) language, merely that identified on the sentence-level by *Lingua-Ident*. According to this, all word tokens of this sentence were predicted to be FR, except for the 3 inside the « and » , which *langid.py* classified correctly as DE (sentence accuracy: 50/78). TBLID, on the other hand, identified more words correctly – getting DE for *Zins* and FR for *Intérêts* as "interest" for the two respective languages. It had 65 out of 78 correct and even recognized *Franz* and *Werthmüller* as NEs.

Another motivation that calls for a refinement of VCCS (from 1877 yearbook):

> [4] **GOLD-lenient:** in_de Vissoye_de_ne_fr erfuhr_de ich_de von_de einem_de Thalkundigen_de , sie_de hätten_de « **mauvaises_fr femmes_fr** » zum_de Schlupfwinkel_de gedient_de , und_de da_de ich_de weiter_de forschte_de , was_de denn_de diese_de « **mauvaises_fr femmes_fr** » verübt_de , erhielt_de ich_de die_de zögernde_de Erklärung_de , es_de seien_de « **sorcières_fr** » gewesen_de .

This sentence was extracted as a possible CS candidate due to their « *mauvaises femmes* » segments.

But VCCS does not handle the segment *«sorcières»*, as it is shorter than 15 characters in length, letting it default into the base language of the sentence (DE). TBLID was able to tag the word *sorcières* with FR. Here we see the feasibility of a word-level LID system. (Score information: both systems get 33 out of 34 correct – TB annotations miss on the word *sorcières*, while TBLID recognizes *Thalkundigen* (a DE compound noun meaning "those who are knowledgeable about the valley") as an NE.)

6.3 OCR errors

Despite the crowdsourcing effort to rectify OCR errors for some yearbooks, OCR errors are still bountiful in the corpus, some of them even form clusters of their own. Our approach could be refined through iterating the clustering procedure, mirroring the two-phase setup in Rabinovich and Wintner (2015)) in which the unsupervised clustering algorithm was run twice – separating genre in the first, and Translationese and Original in the second run. This staged approach might help clean up some of our mixed clusters if we, for example, remove the purer clusters (including these "OCR clusters") from the sample first and then re-cluster the remaining words.

6.4 Contextual Accuracy: Diachronic Corpus

Consider the following sentence snippet from the 1874 yearbook:

> [5] **TBLID:** . . . von_de Bünden_de an_de den_de Wiener_de Congress_en und_de nach_de Mailand_de . . .

EN is a minority language in this corpus. Mislabeled EN words are plentiful in our study as EN data is sparse. The system was, however, clever enough to classify *Congress* as EN, which would have been correct were it not for the fact that the word here is the DE word *Kongress* with an archaic spelling.

7 Conclusion

We have presented a data-driven, self-sufficient, cluster-and-label, simple count distributional approach that identifies the language of word types of a multilingual domain-specific corpus of almost 40 million tokens. We report an accuracy of 89.91%

based on about 5,000 word tokens evaluated and the only "supervision" required was the labor to manually label 50 clusters. We noted some fundamental issues in the definition of gold standard in LID and devised two annotation standards. Different arguments speak for and against various possibilities to optimize the system – the assignment of multiple labels (esp. for multilingual homographs), a more explicit but smart modeling of surrounding context (for example, through combining clustering with HMM model after clustering, or staging clustering itself), and the refinement of the code switching detection algorithm proposed by Volk and Clematide (2014). Through our comparison with off-the-shelf alternatives, we learned that LID of small(er) segments is far from a solved task. Future directions may also include investigating whether incorporating supervised methods would improve performance and testing this method on other datasets.

Acknowledgments

We would like to thank *Text+Berg digital* for sharing their existing code-switching annotations and helpful suggestions. We would also like to thank the three anonymous reviewers for their valuable comments.

References

Kenneth Ward Church and Patrick Hanks. 1990. Word association norms, mutual information, and lexicography. *Computational Linguistics*, 16(1):22–29.

Scott C. Deerwester, Susan T. Dumais, Thomas K. Landauer, George W. Furnas, and Richard A. Harshman. 1990. Indexing by latent semantic analysis. *JASIS*, 41(6):391–407.

Harsh Jhamtani, Suleep Kumar Bhogi, and Vaskar Raychoudhury. 2014. Word-level language identification in bi-lingual code-switched texts. In Wirote Aroonmanakun, Prachya Boonkwan, and Thepchai Supnithi, editors, *Proceedings of the 28th Pacific Asia Conference on Language, Information and Computation, PACLIC 28, Cape Panwa Hotel, Phuket, Thailand, December 12-14, 2014*, pages 348–357. The PACLIC 28 Organizing Committee and PACLIC Steering Committee / ACL / Department of Linguistics, Faculty of Arts, Chulalongkorn University.

Ben King and Steven P. Abney. 2013. Labeling the languages of words in mixed-language documents using weakly supervised methods. In Lucy Vanderwende, Hal Daumé III, and Katrin Kirchhoff, editors, *Human Language Technologies: Conference of the North American Chapter of the Association of Computational Linguistics, Proceedings, June 9-14, 2013, Westin Peachtree Plaza Hotel, Atlanta, Georgia, USA*, pages 1110–1119. The Association for Computational Linguistics.

Omer Levy, Yoav Goldberg, and Ido Dagan. 2015. Improving distributional similarity with lessons learned from word embeddings. *TACL*, 3:211–225.

Marco Lui and Timothy Baldwin. 2012. langid.py: An off-the-shelf language identification tool. In *The 50th Annual Meeting of the Association for Computational Linguistics, Proceedings of the System Demonstrations, July 10, 2012, Jeju Island, Korea*, pages 25–30. The Association for Computer Linguistics.

Marco Lui. 2014. *Generalized language identification*. PhD thesis, The University of Melbourne.

Christopher D. Manning, Prabhakar Raghavan, and Hinrich Schütze. 2008. *Introduction to information retrieval*. Cambridge University Press.

Fabian Pedregosa, Gaël Varoquaux, Alexandre Gramfort, Vincent Michel, Bertrand Thirion, Olivier Grisel, Mathieu Blondel, Peter Prettenhofer, Ron Weiss, Vincent Dubourg, Jake VanderPlas, Alexandre Passos, David Cournapeau, Matthieu Brucher, Matthieu Perrot, and Edouard Duchesnay. 2011. Scikit-learn: Machine learning in python. *Journal of Machine Learning Research*, 12:2825–2830.

Ella Rabinovich and Shuly Wintner. 2015. Unsupervised identification of translationese. *TACL*, 3:419–432.

Thamar Solorio, Elizabeth Blair, Suraj Maharjan, Steven Bethard, Mona Diab, Mahmoud Ghoneim, Abdelati Hawwari, Fahad AlGhamdi, Julia Hirschberg, Alison Chang, and Pascale Fung. 2014. Overview for the first shared task on language identification in code-switched data. In *Proceedings of the First Workshop on Computational Approaches to Code Switching*, pages 62–72, Doha, Qatar, October. Association for Computational Linguistics.

Martin Volk and Simon Clematide. 2014. Detecting code-switching in a multilingual alpine heritage corpus. In *Proceedings of the First Workshop on Computational Approaches to Code Switching*, pages 24–33, Doha, Qatar, October. Association for Computational Linguistics.

Learning Translations for Tagged Words:
Extending the Translation Lexicon of an ITG for Low Resource Languages

Markus Saers and **Dekai Wu**
Human Language Technology Center
Department of Computer Science and Engineering
The Hong Kong University of Science and Technology
HKUST, Clear Water Bay, Kowloon, Hong Kong
{masaers|dekai}@cs.ust.hk

Abstract

We tackle the challenge of learning part-of-speech classified translations as part of an inversion transduction grammar, by learning translations for English words with known part-of-speech tags, both from existing translation lexica and from parallel corpora. When translating from a low resource language into English, we can expect to have rich resources for English, such as treebanks, and small amounts of bilingual resources, such as translation lexica and parallel corpora. We solve the problem of integrating these heterogeneous resources into a single model using stochastic Inversion Transduction Grammars, which we augment with wildcards to handle unknown translations.

1 Introduction

We introduce an augmentation to Inversion Transduction Grammars, or ITGs (Wu, 1997), that allow us to under specify the translation of lexical rules, and defer to observed usage to decide, within the syntactic context of the lexical rule, how the wildcard should be instantiated. Having specific wildcard rules instead of just instantiating all possible translations for the sentence pair at hand (a) allows us to use it as a back-off: we can limit the use of these spurious rules to the circumstances when we have no other choice, and (b) allows us to explicitly reserve some probability mass for the unknown translations of a lexical unit, which also gives us a hint about how certain we are about the known translations. This allows us to say things like "we know that twelve is a cardinal number but it's not in our

translation lexicon, let's see what it is translated to in the parallel corpus". Whith small amounts of data, it is imperative to get the structural generalizations right in order to get adequate statistics; there simply aren't enough examples of longer chunks to get reliable counts. This approach allows us to make good use of the limited parallel resources that are available in a way that traditional statistical machine translation systems are unable to; and to make good use of the human translation examples in a way that traditional rule-based machine translation systems are unable to. Even statistical tree-based models typically require word alignments as input, which again requires large amounts of parallel data to learn well. In contrast, Inversion Transduction Grammars learn the translation model and the word alignments simultaneously, effectively integrating over all possible alignments during training. This is possible because of the strong modeling bias, that limits the search space of possible compositions to make the seemingly intractable problem of bilingual composition tractable, without resorting to heuristics. The modeling bias has been empirically shown to still allows the model to express most structural differences that have been observed between natural languages. Taken together, this lets us mostly rely on what we already know, and incorporate new knowledge as we encounter the need to. This is ideal in the low resource language setting, where we want to stick to presumably hard earned prior knowledge when possible, but still have the option of adding to this knowledge base when needed.

The low-resource language translation setting presumes that we have small amounts of resources in

55

Proceedings of the Workshop on Multilingual and Cross-lingual Methods in NLP, pages 55–64,
San Diego, California, June 17, 2016. ©2016 Association for Computational Linguistics

the input language, and large amounts of resources in the output language (English). The job of a translation system is to produce fluent output that adequately represents the meaning of the input, so a translation system should be biased towards the output language. We do this by basing our ITG model on an English treebank, which allows us to (a) extract a binarized context-free grammar, CFG, and (b) estimate initial probabilities for the structural rules. The stochastic CFG can then be mirrored to form a grammatical channel model (Wu and Wong, 1998).

Conventional statistical machine translation, or SMT, systems such as phrase-based SMT rely on large amounts of parallel data to collect statistics over how large chunks translate between two languages. These models are highly specific, and may have two different rules for example, for a long and complicated noun phrase with the determiner and for the very same noun phrase without it. Needless to say this kind of modeling is too wasteful to be of much use when there is very small amounts of parallel data available. Tree-based models, models that allow for chunks containing general categories as opposed to fully lexicalized chunks, are better able to generalize, but make poor use of the data by disregarding translations that fall outside of the single monolingually motivated parse tree that has been committed to. A forest-based system would alleviate this problem, but two problems still remain: The conventional systems all take a preexisting word alignment as input, disregarding anything that does not conform to it. And none of them make use of forests in the *output* language.

In contrast to conventional systems, our proposed model jointly models the parse forest of the output language, the lexical alignment to the input language, and thus also the projection of the output language parse forest onto the input language sentence, as well as the structural differences needed to make this projection happen. All of this is possible because of ITGs: Their inductive bias allows us to disregard huge swathes of the search space when explaining the structural differences. Their similarity with CFGs allows us to use an English context-free grammar as a starting point for induction. And their computational complexity allows us to efficiently collect rule expectations.

The presented model is capable of exploring the entire space of structural differences between, in our case, English and Chinese, that conform to (a) the English CFG, and (b) the ITG-constraints. It is also capable of expanding the translation dictionary beyond what we initialize it with to cover the small parallel corpus that we assume is available. Although Chinese is by no means a low resource language, it is vastly different from English, meaning that there are plenty of structural differences to learn. We also allow very limited Chinese resources in building our model, simulating a low resource language setting.

Inversion transductions are formally a family of transductions, where a transduction is the bilingual version of a formal language, such that it relates two formal languages to each other. Inversion transductions are generated by Inversion Transduction Grammars, or ITGs (Wu, 1997), which share several traits with CFGs in that the transduction rules have single non-terminals on the left-hand side, and in that there is always a 2-normal form equivalence for every ITG. The latter is quite rare for transduction grammars, and limits the structural differences that can be generated between the languages. These limits in structural differences have been empirically shown to include most of the differences found between natural languages (Søgaard and Wu, 2009), and make efficient processing possible.

Formally, an ITG is a tuple $\langle \mathcal{N}, \mathcal{W}_0, \mathcal{W}_1, \mathcal{R}, S \rangle$, where $\mathcal{N}$ is a finite nonempty set of nonterminals, $\mathcal{W}_0$ is a finite set of terminals in the output language L_0, $\mathcal{W}_1$ is a finite set of terminals in the input language L_1, $\mathcal{R}$ is a finite nonempty set of inversion transduction rules and $S \in \mathcal{N}$ is a designated start symbol. An inversion transduction rule is restricted to take one of the following forms:

$$ S \to [A], \quad A \to [\varphi^+], \quad A \to \langle \varphi^+ \rangle $$

where $S \in \mathcal{N}$ is the start symbol, $A \in \mathcal{N}$ is a nonterminal, and φ^+ is a nonempty sequence of nonterminals and biterminals. A biterminal is a pair: $\mathcal{W}_0^* \times \mathcal{W}_1^*$, where at least one of the strings have to be nonempty. The square and angled brackets signal straight and inverted order respectively. The brackets are frequently left out when there is only one element on the right-hand side.

The ITG 2-normal form is analogous to the Chomsky normal form for CFGs, where the rules are further restricted to only the following forms:

$$S \to A, \quad A \to [BC], \quad A \to \langle BC \rangle,$$
$$A \to e/f, \quad A \to e/\epsilon, \quad A \to \epsilon/f$$

where $S \in \mathcal{N}$ is the start symbol, $A, B, C \in \mathcal{N}$ are nonterminals, $e \in \mathcal{W}_0$ is an L_0 token, $f \in \mathcal{W}_1$ is an L_1 token, and ϵ is the empty token.

A bracketing ITG, or BITG, has only one nonterminal symbol (other than the dedicated start symbol), which means that the nonterminals carry no information at all other than the fact that their yields are discrete unit.

2   Related work

The use of structure as input to the training of a statistical model in machine translation was pioneered by Yamada and Knight (2001), where they extend the IBM model 1 (Brown *et al.*, 1993) to incorporate syntactic features derived from a parse tree on the output language (the input to the noisy channel, but the output of the decoder). The generative story of the model is that an English parse tree has the children of its nodes reordered, gets the option to insert a foreign token to the left or right of any node, and finally have all the English leaf nodes translated. Reading the leaf nodes of the tree in order yields the generated foreign sentence. Being a generative model, it is straight forward to train using EM, which they do. Manual evaluation shows that the word alignments corresponding to the one-best derivation are better than those of IBM model 5, and that they managed to get 10 out of the evaluated 50 sentence pairs perfectly aligned, whereas IBM model 5 got none. There are two key differences between Yamada and Knight (2001) and out model: (a) Their model describes how a foreign sentence is generated from an English parse tree, our model describes how sentence pairs are jointly generated. And (b) their model requires committing to a single English parse tree, our model jointly parses and aligns the sentences, effectively integrating out all parse trees that our grammar allows for the English sentence.

Perhaps the most prolific translation model that involves trees is Galley *et al.* (2004), which learns very complex rules such as (ne VB pas) $\to$ (VP (AUX does) (RB not) x_2) where x_2 is a variable binding to the second element in the left-hand side. The method takes a parallel sentence pair where one of the sentences has been parsed, and a word alignment, and produces, for each observed word aligned sentence pair, the minimal set of rules to explain it. This method allows complicated rules to be extracted, and different feature scores to be calculated for the extracted rules. This does, however, come at the cost of not being able to optimize the model in any meaningful way. Instead, one has to resort to tuning the feature weights used by the decoder. Any mistakes made by the parser or the automatic word aligner are incorporated into the model without any recourse. In contrast, our model jointly parses the output language and aligns the sentences, within a generative model that can be optimized globally across the entire training data.

It is possible to alleviate the mismatch between given alignments and parse trees. Riesa and Marcu (2010) formulate a discriminative k-best alignment model with hundreds of features that can be used to choose the best alignment that matches a given tree. The method as presented require some analysis on both input and output language for the feature model, as well as a set of hand aligned sentences for training; neither of which are readily available for low resource languages. Similarly, DeNero and Klein (2007) describe a model to tailor word alignments to existing syntactic trees; in our model, we instead consider all possible trees allowed by a CFG. Burkett *et al.* (2010) and Burkett and Klein (2012) take the opposite approach and alter the trees to fit the alignments, as presented, their approach requires parallel treebanks to train on, which cannot be expected to be available when translating to or from a low resource language.

It is also possible to learn translation rules focusing on the syntax of the input language rather than output language. Huang *et al.* (2006) turn the tables, and learn translation rules with the input language parsed. Their approach forces the decoder to commit to a single input tree and then build possible output *strings* rather than building possible output *trees*. The model has also been generalized so that rules can be extracted from input forests rather than single trees (Mi and Huang, 2008), and the decoder has been extended to accept forests as input (Mi *et al.*, 2008). The rule extraction process still requires a word alignment to be provided. Since our model is based on a grammar rather than parse trees, it essentially integrates out all trees as well as the alignments needed to perform the rule extraction. There is a difference in that we have an output language grammar, but we still implicitly build input language forests.

Our model is related to the grammatical channel model of Wu and Wong (1998) in that the way we set up our initial grammar is similar, but where they then proceed to translate directly with it, induction has just started with our model. Key differences is that they merely mirror structural rules, allowing them to be completely straight or completely inverted, and that they make no effort to extend the translation dictionary. In contrast, we allow long rules to be broken down, which allows for more differences in word order, and induce additional lexical translations that are helpful in explaining the training data.

3   Induction Algorithm

The main focus of this paper is to learn translations of known English lexical units. Our method relies on being able to realize when it lacks the translation needed to use an English lexical unit in a specific syntactic context, and to find viable candidate translations from the observed sentence pair. The model knows which English tokens go where (from the treebank), and can be expected to have some translation vocabulary, mainly of content words (from the translation lexicon). It can easily realize when it lacks an applicable translation, and if there is an applicable wildcard-rule we allow it to hypothesize a realization of that wildcard from the current situation. This is a good mechanism for extending the translation lexicon for content words, but it requires the biparser to determine the syntactic context that this hypothesizing takes place in. This in turn requires the English structural rules to be adapted so that they can handle Chinese as well. To do this, we hypothesize that there are two main differences between English and Chinese: word order and function words. It makes sense for most content words to have some kind of correspondence in the other language, but they rarely occur in the same order. The function words, on the other hand are sometimes realized in both languages, but frequently one language will use a function word, whereas the other language will ignore that distinction, or realize it

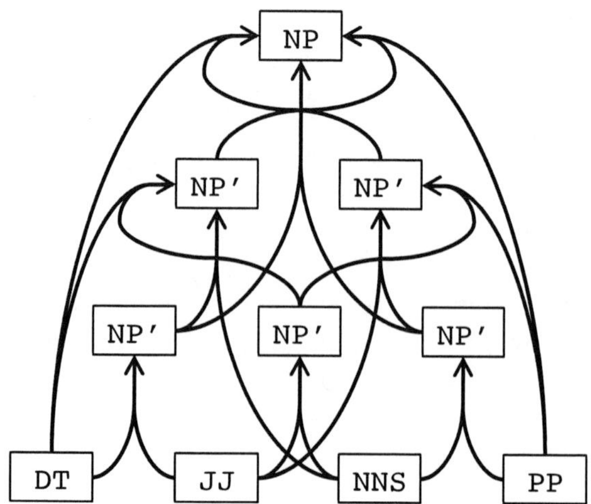

Figure 1:   All possible binarization of a structural rule with four constituents. Any valid hyperpath from the four leaves to the root constitute a valid binarization.

through word order or in some other syntactic way. An example of the former is the Chinese question particle (吗), which is realized in English through the syntactic question construction. An example of the latter is determinate case in English, which is simply not realized in Chinese, meaning that the word the needs to be intelligently inserted when translating from Chinese to English.

To account for the word order differences, we binarize the structural rules, allowing each binary rule to be either straight or inverted. This allows the model to account for any word order difference within the ITG-constraints. Since the model is already heavily biased towards English, allowing English words to not translate into anything takes care of the case where there is no Chinese equivalence of an English function word. For the Chinese function words, there either is an English equivalence, in which case the mechanism for content words will find it, or there isn't, in which case we simply allow the biparser to algorithmically skip these words.

3.1   Step 1

Like Wu and Wong (1998) we start with an English grammar and a translation dictionary. But, where they allow structural rules to be either completely straight or completely inverted, we allow *any binarization* of the structural rules to be either straight or inverted. And, where they allow any English word

Table 1: The result of converting the two English CFG rules JJ → *nice* and NP → DT JJ NNS PP to ITG rules using our proposed method and that of Wu and Wong (1998). Clubs are wild, and NP′ is the auxiliary symbol for NP.

Our method			Wu and Wong (1998)
JJ → *nice*/和蔼	NP → [DT NP′]	NP → ⟨DT NP′⟩	
JJ → *nice*/可亲	NP → [NP′ NP′]	NP → ⟨NP′ NP′⟩	
JJ → *nice*/♣	NP → [NP′ PP]	NP → ⟨NP′ PP⟩	
	NP′ → [DT NP′]	NP′ → ⟨DT NP′⟩	JJ → *nice*/和蔼
	NP′ → [JJ NP′]	NP′ → ⟨JJ NP′⟩	JJ → *nice*/可亲
	NP′ → [NP′ PP]	NP′ → ⟨NP′ PP⟩	NP → [DT JJ NNS PP]
	NP′ → [NP′ NNS]	NP′ → ⟨NP′ NNS⟩	NP → ⟨DT JJ NNS PP⟩
	NP′ → [DT JJ]	NP′ → ⟨DT JJ⟩	
	NP′ → [JJ NNS]	NP′ → ⟨JJ NNS⟩	
	NP′ → [NNS PP]	NP′ → ⟨NNS PP⟩	

to translate into whatever the translation dictionary mandates, we additionally assume that any English word can translate into a wildcard token that represents the translations not in the dictionary. When binarizing rules, there are many approaches one could take. It is possible to "box" nonterminals to produce an exactly equivalent binary grammar. Boxing means replacing any right-hand side occurrence of a sequence, eg. DT NN with a single boxed nonterminal $\overline{\text{DT NN}}$, which deterministically expand to the original sequence with the rule $\overline{\text{DT NN}}$ → DT NN. This tends to expand the set of nonterminals needlessly, and differentiating, for example, between the case when a noun phrase contains three versus four nouns is counter-productively specific. Instead, we opt to have each left-hand side symbol be associated with one auxiliary symbol that handles the binarization of that category, and represents a fragment of it. We essentially generate the entire parse forest rooted in the left-hand side, with the right-hand side symbols as the leaves, and every internal node labeled with the auxiliary symbol (see Figure 1). From this parse forest of the rule, we can extract all binary rules, and add a straight and an inverted version of them to our ITG. This allows us to account for any permutation of the right-hand sides that fall within the ITG-constraints. Table 1 shows the result of applying our method as opposed to applying the method of Wu and Wong (1998) to the two English CFG-rules NP → DT JJ NNS PP and JJ → *nice*.

3.2 Step 2

At this point our model has too many structural rules and too few lexical rules, so the next step is to root out the superfluous structural rules and build out the coverage of the lexical rules. We do this by reestimating the ITG using a small parallel corpus and variational Bayes; to weed out unnecessary structural rules we use a sparse prior, and to build out the lexical coverage, we hypothesis that the wild card will be binding predominantly to valid translations of the associated English word, and instantiate the observed bindings into the ITG.

Variational Bayes is mechanically similar to expectation maximization (Dempster *et al.*, 1977) with inside-outside (Lari and Young, 1990), but optimizes the maximum *a posteriori* probability of the model given the data and a prior, rather than the maximum likelihood of the model given the data. Intuitively it can be understood as collecting the fractional counts, or expectations, from the data and discounting them before maximizing. Given that we have rule expectations from inside-outside $E(A → \varphi)$, the reestimated probability of a rule is:

$$p(A → \varphi) = \frac{e^{\psi\left(E(A→\varphi)+\alpha_{A→\varphi}\right)}}{\sum_{\phi} e^{\psi\left(E(A→\phi)+\alpha_{A→\phi}\right)}}$$

where ψ is the digamma function, and $\alpha_{A→\varphi}$ is the prior of the rule $A → \varphi$ (Kurihara and Sato, 2006). It has previously been used for ITG learning (Zhang *et al.*, 2008; Saers and Wu, 2013), but only with uniform priors. In this paper, we distinguish three different classes of rules, and assign them different priors: *preexisting lexical rules, lexical rules with wild-cards*, and *other rules*. We want the preexisting lexical rules to have a relatively high prior, since we trust our translation dictionary. We may or may not want to keep the wildcard rules, and having a separate prior for them allows us to easily choose their fate. All other rules need to earn their keep, and are thus subjected to a sparse prior.

The lexical coverage is extended by hypothesizing that what the wildcard binds to in the expectation collection phase constitutes a valid translation. This is an iterative step, where we first biparse the parallel corpus with the previous ITG. The wildcard is allowed to match a preset number of Chinese tokens when no known translation applies, and we also allow skipping both English and Chinese tokens as a backoff. Once a sentence pair has been processed, we inspect the parse forest and extract all bindings for all wildcards and instantiate the corresponding rules with half of the fractional counts it would have had if it existed. The other half of the fractional counts is retained with the wildcard rule.

The biparser we have is based on Saers *et al.* (2009), with the addition of wildcard matching and skipping. The algorithm is very suitable for our needs, as it approximates the search to bring down the time complexity of collecting the fractional counts from $O(n^6)$ to $O(bn^3)$, where n is proportional to the length of the sentences in the pair, and b is the width of the search beam (the wider the beam, the more accurate the approximation). We implement skipping as implicit, low probability rules on the following forms:

$$A \rightarrow [A\ \epsilon/f], \quad A \rightarrow [\epsilon/f\ A],$$
$$A \rightarrow [A\ e/\epsilon], \quad A \rightarrow [e/\epsilon\ A]$$

This allows the parser to maintain the category, but consume a foreign or English token adjacent to a known constituent. The low probability makes the parser avoid skipping if possible.

4 Experimental Setup

To test the induction algorithm, we empirically compare the results of our proposed system to a bracketing ITG induced from the same parallel corpus, but without any prior knowledge of English. To extract a CFG over English, we use the Penn treebank

(Marcus *et al.*, 1993), with relative frequencies of the productions as the rule probabilities. As translation dictionary, we use the *Chinese–English Translation Lexicon*(Huang and Graff, 2002). When transforming the CFG into an ITG (Section 3.1) we divide the probability mass of the CFG-rules uniformly among the ITG rules they spawn.

As the small parallel data set we use the IWSLT07 Chinese–English data set (Fordyce, 2007), which contains 46,867 sentence pairs. Chinese sentence are typically written without spaces, so we use a tool (Wu, 1999) to segment it into more "word like" units. We allow the wildcard to match zero or one such Chinese tokens. To make use of the parallel data, we perform 10 iterations of reestimation (Section 3.2), with a beam width $b = 100$, and the following priors: preexisting lexical rules: 10^{-2}, lexical rules with wildcards: 10^{-5}, other rules: 10^{-10}. We qualitatively evaluate the resulting ITG by looking at how it explains some of the parallel sentences, as opposed to how the baseline bracketing ITG explains them.

5 Results

We evaluate the results qualitatively, by comparing the output of our induced system with that of the baseline BITG. Figures 2 and 4 contain the output of our system, and Figures 3 and 5 contain the output of the baseline BITG. All Figures have the same structure: the English sentence on the top; the Chinese sentence on the left; a compositional alignment matrix between them where black boxes represent correct terminals, gray boxes represent incorrect terminals and outlined boxes represent the compositions; and the corresponding ITG parse tree over the English sentence.

Figure 2 shows a single noun phrase utterance (room fifty-six twelve. translating into 五六一二房。 'five six one two room.') taken from our training data, as biparsed by our induced ITG. The tokens align well, which would not have been possible if the Chinese segmenter hadn't grouped 一 'one' and 二 'two' together as a single token for twelve to align with. It also aligns fifty to 五 'five', which is technically wrong, but may be useful when different languages prefer to group numbers differently. Notice that the noun phrase needs to separate the number series from the noun (room) in order to flip the or-

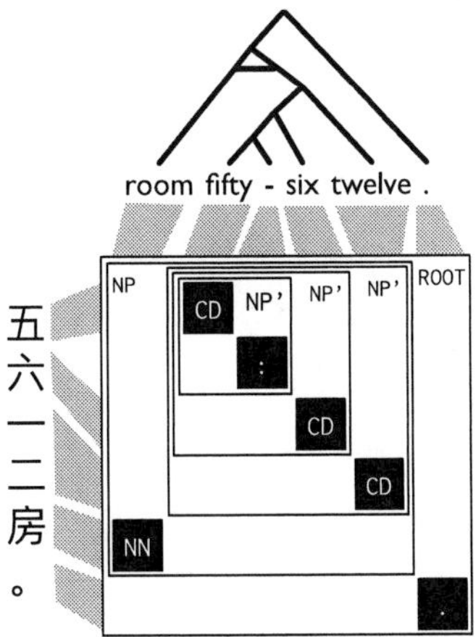

Figure 2: The tree structure imposed on one of the training sentences by our induced ITG.

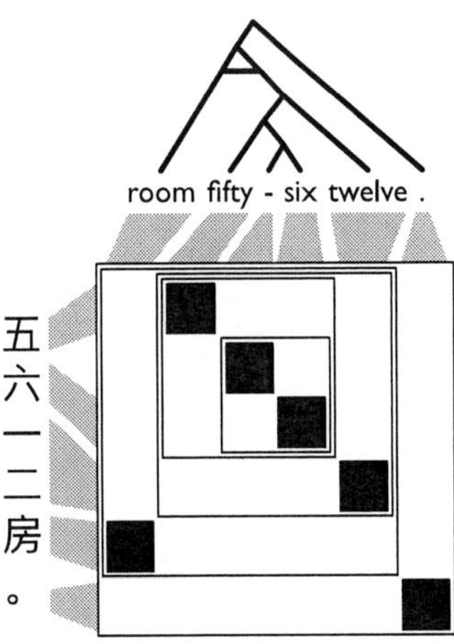

Figure 3: The tree structure imposed on one of the training sentences by the baseline bracketing ITG.

der in Chinese. It has also chosen to make the NP′ a right-heavy tree, when it could very well have made it left-heavy or balanced. This is desirable, since it appears to have generalized arbitrarily long chains of numbers, so what it has learned is that a noun-phrase fragment can consist of a noun-phrase fragment and a number. Inspecting the grammar, we find the following relevant rules:

$$\text{NP}' \overset{6.4\%}{\to} [\text{CD NP}'] \quad \text{NP}' \overset{4.8\%}{\to} \langle \text{CD NP}' \rangle$$
$$\text{NP}' \overset{1.4\%}{\to} [\text{NP}' \text{ CD}] \quad \text{NP}' \overset{1.2\%}{\to} \langle \text{NP}' \text{ CD} \rangle$$

There is a clear bias in favor of right-heavy trees (the first two rules account for about 11.2% of noun-phrase fragments, as opposed to 2.6% which are left-heavy), as well as a bias for maintaining the order of number sequences in noun-phrase fragments (7.8% as opposed to 6%).

The bracketing ITG does not know what to do in these circumstances. As Figure 3 shows, the number sequence is arbitrarily nested. It is possible to force an ITG to always prefer a canonical left- or right-heavy sequence of straight (or inverted) rule applications, but that is an external constraint put on it manually. We managed to induce that preference automatically.

The second sentence pair is the question how long does it take to reach Japan? with its Chinese translation 到日本要花多长时间? 'reach Japan need spend how long time?'. Notice that this is a very hard translation to recreate for an automatic system. English

mandates a subject in well-formed clauses, Chinese does not; English requires an auxiliary verb in questions, Chinese does not; English requires an infinitive marker, Chinese does not; English allows time to be implicit from how long, Chinese requires it to be explicit.

Figure 4 shows our system, and Figure 5 shows the BITG. Our system has learned that English has a mandatory subject, which Chinese lacks, as is evident from it begin correctly classified as a pronoun, and translated into nothing, whereas the BITG has it incorrectly translated as 花 'spend'. Our system has incorrectly aligned does to 多 'how', whereas the BITG has it incorrectly aligned it to 时间 'time'. Our system has correctly classified to as an infinitive marker as opposed to a preposition, but aligned it with 到 'reach', whereas the BITG has is correctly aligned to nothing. It is, however worth noting that our system has managed to compose to reach Japan as a unit, whereas the BITG has no concept of an infinitive verb at all. The treebank we extract our grammar from has no specific category for infinitive verb phrases either, but our system has repurposed the S-7 category (that occurs in the treebank, but not it's annotation guidelines) to represent infinitive verb phrases. Both systems have incorrectly aligned 时间 'time' to something.

Looking at the nestings, it becomes clear that the BITG has done a good job of nailing the token-to-token correspondences, but that the structure is all wrong. It is a left-heavy tree where one would ex-

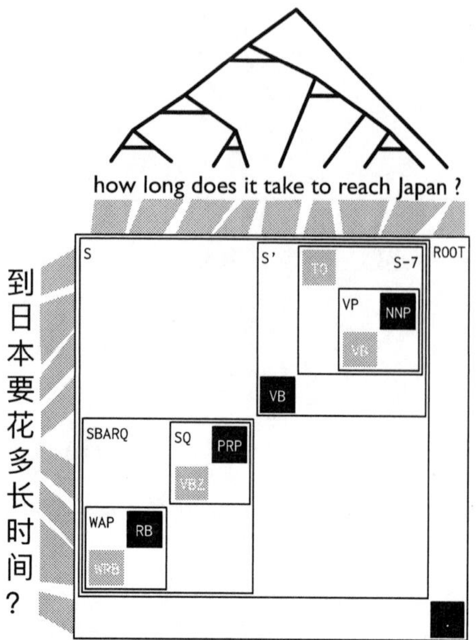

Figure 4: The tree structure imposed on one of the training sentences by our induced ITG.

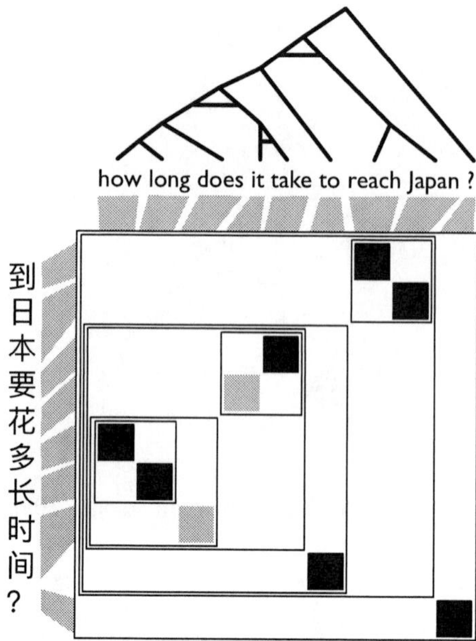

Figure 5: The tree structure imposed on one of the training sentences by the baseline bracketing ITG.

pect a mostly right-heavy tree. Our system does a better job with the nesting, although one would have wished to see take to reach Japan be dominated by how long does it, rather than being on the same level. The spans are also reasonably well labeled.

6 Conclusions

We have presented a novel approach to low-resource language translation that relies on extending the lexical coverage of a linguistically informed inversion transduction grammar. The linguistic information is derived from an output language treebank, and extending the translation lexicon requires the correct translation for a word with a specific part-of-speech tag to be identified. We have shown a way of doing precisely that through setting aside part of the probability mass for unknown translations, represented as wildcards in the ITG. Staying within the formalism of ITGs is desirable, as they can be trained directly on parallel data, without the need to first induce, and commit to, a single word alignment. The inductive bias of the ITG formalism allows us to integrate over all relevant word alignments in polynomial time, while still being able to capture most of the structural variation observed between human languages. It also allows us to combine multiple heterogenous sources of knowledge, in this paper we used (a) a context-free grammar derived from an English treebank, (b) a Chinese–English translation dictionary, and (c) a small Chinese–English parallel corpus, which is imperative in a low-resource language setting, where all available resources need to be utilized.

Acknowledgements

This material based upon work supported in part by the Defense Advanced Research Projects Agency (DARPA) under LORELEI contract HR0011-15-C-0114, BOLT contracts HR0011-12-C-0014 and HR0011-12-C-0016, and GALE contracts HR0011-06-C-0022 and HR0011-06-C-0023; by the European Union under the Horizon 2020 grant agreement 645452 (QT21) and FP7 grant agreement 287658; and by the Hong Kong Research Grants Council (RGC) research grants GRF16210714, GRF16214315, GRF620811 and GRF621008. Any opinions, findings and conclusions or recommendations expressed in this material are those of the authors and do not necessarily reflect the views of DARPA, the EU, or RGC.

References

Peter F. Brown, Stephen A. Della Pietra, Vincent J. Della Pietra, and Robert L. Mercer. The mathematics of machine translation: Parameter estimation. *Computational Linguistics*, 19(2):263–311, 1993.

David Burkett and Dan Klein. Transforming trees to improve syntactic convergence. In *Proceedings of the 2012 Joint Conference on Empirical Methods in Natural Language Processing and Computational Natural Language Learning*, pages 863–872, Jeju Island, Korea, July 2012. Association for Computational Linguistics.

David Burkett, John Blitzer, and Dan Klein. Joint parsing and alignment with weakly synchronized grammars. In *Human Language Technologies: The 2010 Annual Conference of the North American Chapter of the Association for Computational Linguistics (NAACL HLT 2010)*, pages 127–135, Los Angeles, California, June 2010.

Arthur Pentland Dempster, Nan M. Laird, and Donald Bruce Rubin. Maximum likelihood from incomplete data via the EM algorithm. *Journal of the Royal Statistical Society. Series B (Methodological)*, 39(1):1–38, 1977.

John DeNero and Dan Klein. Tailoring word alignments to syntactic machine translation. In *Proceedings of the 45th Annual Meeting of the Association of Computational Linguistics*, pages 17–24, Prague, Czech Republic, June 2007. Association for Computational Linguistics.

C. S. Fordyce. Overview of the IWSLT 2007 evaluation campaign. In *International Workshop on Spoken Language Translation (IWSLT 2007)*, pages 1–12, 2007.

Michel Galley, Mark Hopkins, Kevin Knight, and Daniel Marcu. What's in a translation rule? In *HLT-NAACL 2004: Main Proceedings*, pages 273–280, Boston, Massachusetts, May 2004.

Shudong Huang and David Graff. Chinese–English translation lexicon version 3.0 LDC2002L27, 2002.

Liang Huang, Kevin Knight, and Aravind Joshi. Statistical syntax-directed translation with extended domain of locality. In *7th Biennial Conference*

Association for Machine Translation in the Americas (AMTA 2006), pages 66–73, Boston, Massachusetts, 2006.

Kenichi Kurihara and Taisuke Sato. Variational bayesian grammar induction for natural language. In *Proceedings of the 8th International Conference on Grammatical Inference: Algorithms and Applications*, ICGI'06, pages 84–96, Berlin, Heidelberg, 2006. Springer-Verlag.

Karim Lari and Steve J. Young. The estimation of stochastic context-free grammars using the inside-outside algorithm. *Computer Speech & Language*, 4(1):35–56, 1990.

Mitchell P. Marcus, Mary Ann Marcinkiewicz, and Beatrice Santorini. Building a large annotated corpus of english: The penn treebank. *Computational Linguistics*, 19(2):313–330, June 1993.

Haitao Mi and Liang Huang. Forest-based translation rule extraction. In *2008 Conference on Empirical Methods in Natural Language Processing (EMNLP 2008)*, pages 206–214, Honolulu, Hawaii, October 2008.

Haitao Mi, Liang Huang, and Qun Liu. Forest-based translation. In *46th Annual Meeting of the Association for Computational Linguistics: Human Language Technologies (ACL-08: HLT)*, pages 192–199, Columbus, Ohio, June 2008.

Jason Riesa and Daniel Marcu. Hierarchical search for word alignment. In *48th Annual Meeting of the Association for Computational Linguistics (ACL 2010)*, pages 157–166, Uppsala, Sweden, July 2010.

Markus Saers and Dekai Wu. Bayesian induction of bracketing inversion transduction grammars. In *Sixth International Joint Conference on Natural Language Processing (IJCNLP2013)*, pages 1158–1166, Nagoya, Japan, October 2013. Asian Federation of Natural Language Processing.

Markus Saers, Joakim Nivre, and Dekai Wu. Learning stochastic bracketing inversion transduction grammars with a cubic time biparsing algorithm. In *11th International Conference on Parsing Technologies (IWPT'09)*, pages 29–32, Paris, France, October 2009.

Anders Søgaard and Dekai Wu. Empirical lower bounds on translation unit error rate for the full class of inversion transduction grammars. In *Proceedings of the 11th International Conference on Parsing Technologies (IWPT'09)*, pages 33–36, Paris, France, October 2009.

Dekai Wu and Hongsing Wong. Machine translation with a stochastic grammatical channel. In *36th Annual Meeting of the Association for Computational Linguistics and 17th International Conference on Computational Linguistics (COLING-ACL '98)*, volume 2, pages 1408–1415, Montreal, Quebec, August 1998.

Dekai Wu. Stochastic inversion transduction grammars and bilingual parsing of parallel corpora. *Computational Linguistics*, 23(3):377–403, 1997.

Zhibiao Wu. LDC Chinese segmenter, 1999.

Kenji Yamada and Kevin Knight. A syntax-based statistical translation model. In *39th Annual Meeting of the Association for Computational Linguistics and 10th Conference of the European Chapter of the Association for Computational Linguistics*, pages 523–530, Toulouse, France, July 2001.

Hao Zhang, Chris Quirk, Robert C. Moore, and Daniel Gildea. Bayesian learning of non-compositional phrases with synchronous parsing. In *46th Annual Meeting of the Association for Computational Linguistics: Human Language Technologies (ACL-08: HLT)*, pages 97–105, Columbus, Ohio, June 2008.

Comparing Fifty Natural Languages and Twelve Genetic Languages Using Word Embedding Language Divergence (WELD) as a Quantitative Measure of Language Distance

Ehsaneddin Asgari and **Mohammad R.K. Mofrad**
Departments of Bioengineering
University of California, Berkeley
Berkeley, CA 94720, USA
`asgari@ischool.berkeley.edu, mofrad@berkeley.edu`

Abstract

We introduce a new measure of distance between languages based on word embedding, called word embedding language divergence (WELD). WELD is defined as divergence between unified similarity distribution of words between languages. Using such a measure, we perform language comparison for fifty natural languages and twelve genetic languages. Our natural language dataset is a collection of sentence-aligned parallel corpora from bible translations for fifty languages spanning a variety of language families. Although we use parallel corpora, which guarantees having the same content in all languages, interestingly in many cases languages within the same family cluster together. In addition to natural languages, we perform language comparison for the coding regions in the genomes of 12 different organisms (4 plants, 6 animals, and two human subjects). Our result confirms a significant high-level difference in the genetic language model of humans/animals versus plants. The proposed method is a step toward defining a quantitative measure of similarity between languages, with applications in languages classification, genre identification, dialect identification, and evaluation of translations.

1 Introduction

Classification of language varieties is one of the prominent problems in linguistics (Smith, 2016). The term language variety can refer to different styles, dialects, or even a distinct language (Marjorie and Rees-Miller, 2001). It has been a long-standing argument that strictly quantitative methods can be applied to determine the degree of similarity or dissimilarity between languages (Kroeber and Chrétien, 1937; Sankaran et al., 1950; Krámský, 1959; McMahon and McMahon, 2003). The methods proposed in the 1990's and early 2000' mostly relied on utilization of intensive linguistic resources. For instance, similarity between two languages was defined based on the number of common cognates or phonological patterns according to a manually extracted list (Kroeber and Chrétien, 1937; McMahon and McMahon, 2003). Such an approach, of course, is not easily extensible to problems involving new languages. Recently, statistical methods have been proposed to automatically detect cognates (Berg-Kirkpatrick and Klein, 2010; Hall and Klein, 2010; Bouchard-Côté et al., 2013; Ciobanu and Dinu, 2014) and subsequently compare languages based on the number of common cognates (Ciobanu and Dinu, 2014).

In this paper our aim is to define a quantitative measure of distance between languages. Such a metric should reasonably take both syntactic and semantic variability of languages into account. A measure of distance between languages can have various applications including quantitative genetic/typological language classification, styles and genres identification, and translation evaluation. In addition, comparing the biological languages generating the genome in different organisms can potentially shed light on important biological facts.

1.1 Problem Definition

Our goal is to be able to provide a quantitative estimate of distance for any two given languages. In our framework, we define a language as a weighted

Proceedings of the Workshop on Multilingual and Cross-lingual Methods in NLP, pages 65–74,
San Diego, California, June 17, 2016. ©2016 Association for Computational Linguistics

graph $\Omega_L(V, e)$, where V is a set of vertices (words), and $e : (V \times V) \to \Re$ is a weight function mapping a pair of words to their similarity value. Then our goal of approximating the distance between the two languages L and L' can be transferred to the approximation of the distance between $\Omega_L(V, e)$ and $\Omega_{L'}(V', e')$. In order to approach such a problem firstly we need to address the following questions:

- What is a proper weight function e estimating a similarity measure between words $w_i, w_j \in V$ in a language L?
- How can we relate words in V to words in V'?
- And finally, how can we measure a distance between languages Ω_L and $\Omega_{L'}$, which means $D(\Omega_L, \Omega_{L'})$?

In the following section we explain how researchers have addressed the above mentioned questions until now.

1.1.1 Word similarity within a language

The main aim of word similarity methods is to measure how similar pairs of words are to eachother, semantically and syntactically (Han et al., 2013). Such a problem has a wide range of applications in information retrieval, automatic speech recognition, word sense disambiguation, and machine translation (Collobert and Weston, 2008; Glorot et al., 2011; Mikolov et al., 2013c; Turney et al., 2010; Resnik, 1999; Schwenk, 2007).

Various methods have been proposed to measure word similarity, including thesaurus and taxonomy-based approaches, data-driven methods, and hybrid techniques (Miller, 1995; Mohammad and Hirst, 2006; Mikolov et al., 2013a; Han et al., 2013). Taxonomy-based methods are not easily extensible as they usually require extensive human intervention for creation and maintenance (Han et al., 2013). One of the main advantages of data-driven methods is that they can be employed even for domains with shortage of manually annotated data.

Almost all of the data-driven methods such as matrix factorization (Xu et al., 2003), word embedding (Mikolov et al., 2013a), topic models (Blei, 2012), and mutual information (Han et al., 2013) are based on co-occurrences of words within defined units of text data. Each method has its own convention for unit of text, which can be a sentence, paragraph or a sliding window around a word.

Using distributed representations have been one of the most successful approaches for computing word similarity in natural language processing (Collobert et al., 2011). The main idea in distributed representation is characterizing words by the company they keep (Hinton, 1984; Firth, 1975; Collobert et al., 2011).

Recently, continuous vector representations known as word vectors have become popular in natural language processing (NLP) as an efficient approach to represent semantic/syntactic units (Mikolov et al., 2013a; Collobert et al., 2011). Word vectors are trained in the course of training a language model neural network from large amounts of textual data (words and their contexts) (Mikolov et al., 2013a). More precisely, word representations are the outputs of the last hidden layer in a trained neural network for language modeling. Thus, word vectors are supposed to encode the most relevant features to language modeling by observing various samples. In this representation similar words have closer vectors, where similarity is defined in terms of both syntax and semantics. By training word vectors over large corpora of natural languages, interesting patterns have been observed. Words with similar vector representations display multiple types of similarity. For instance, $\overrightarrow{King} - \overrightarrow{Man} + \overrightarrow{Woman}$ is the closest vector to that of the word $\overrightarrow{Queen}$ (an instance of semantic regularities) and $\overrightarrow{quick} - \overrightarrow{quickly} \approx \overrightarrow{slow} - \overrightarrow{slowly}$ (an instance of syntactic regularities). A recent work has proposed the use of word vectors to detect linguistic changes within the same language over time (Kulkarni et al., 2015). The fact that various degrees of similarity were captured by such a representation convinced us to use it as a notion of proximity for words.

1.1.2 Word alignment

As we discussed in section 1.1, in order to compare graphs Ω_L and Ω_L', we need to have a unified definition of words (vertices). Thus, we need to find a mapping function from the words in V to the words in V'. Obviously when two languages have the same vocabulary set this step can be skipped, which is the case when we perform within-language genres analysis or linguistic drifts study (Stamatatos et al., 2000; Kulkarni et al., 2015), or even when we compare biological languages (DNA or protein languages) for different species (Asgari and Mofrad, 2015). However, when our goal is to compare distributional similarity of words for two different languages, such as French and German, we need to find a mapping from words in French to German words.

Finding a word mapping function between two languages can be achieved using a dictionary or using statistical word alignment in parallel corpora (Och and Ney, 2003; Lardilleux and Lepage, 2009). Statistical word alignment is a vital component in any statistical machine translation pipeline (Fraser and Marcu, 2007). Various methods/tools has been proposed for word alignment, such as GIZA++ (Och, 2003) and Anymalign (Lardilleux and Lepage, 2009), which are able to extract high quality word alignments from sentence-aligned multilingual parallel corpora.

One of the data resources we use in this project is a large collection of sentence-aligned parallel corpora we extract from bible translations in fifty languages. Thus, in order to find a word mapping function among all these languages we used statistical word alignment techniques and in particular Anymalign (Lardilleux and Lepage, 2009), which can process any number of languages at once.

1.1.3 Network Analysis of Languages

The rather intuitive approach of treating languages as networks of words has been proposed and explored in the last decade by a number of researchers (i Cancho and Solé, 2001; Liu and Cong, 2013; Cong and Liu, 2014; Gao et al., 2014). In these works, human languages, like many other aspects of human behavior, are modeled as complex networks (Costa et al., 2011), where the nodes are essentially the words of the language and the weights on the edges are calculated based on the co-occurrences of the words (Liu and Cong, 2013; i Cancho and Solé, 2001; Gao et al., 2014). Clustering of 14 languages based on various parameters of a complex network such as average degree, average path length, clustering coefficient, network centralization, diameter, and network heterogeneity has been done by (Liu and Cong, 2013). A similar approach is suggested by (Gao et al., 2014) for analysis of the complexity of six languages. Although, all of the above mentioned methods have presented promising results about similarity and regularity of languages, to our understanding they need the following improvements:

Measure of word similarity: Considering co-occurrences as a measure of similarity between nodes, which is the basis of the above mentioned complex network methods, is a naive estimate of similarity, (Liu and Cong, 2013; i Cancho and Solé, 2001; Gao et al., 2014). The most trivial cases are synonyms, which we expect to be marked as the most similar words to each other. However, since they can only be used interchangeably with each other in the same sentences, their co-occurrences rate is very low. Thus, raw co-occurrence is not necessarily a good indicator of similarity.

Independent vs. joint analysis: Previous methods have compared the parameters of language graphs independently, except for some relatively small networks of words for illustration (Liu and Cong, 2013; i Cancho and Solé, 2001; Gao et al., 2014). However, two languages may have similar settings of the edges but for completely different concepts. Thus, a systematic way for joint comparison of these networks is essential.

Language collection: The previous analysis was performed on a relatively small number of languages. For instance in (Liu and Cong, 2013), fourteen languages were studied where twelve of them were from the Slavic family of languages, and (Gao et al., 2014) studied six languages. Clearly, studying more languages from a broader set of language families would be more indicative.

1.2 Our Contributions

In this paper, we suggest a heuristic method toward a quantitative measure of distance between languages. We propose divergence between unified similarity distribution of words as a quantitative measure of distance between languages.

Measure of word similarity: We use cosine similarity between word vectors as the metric of word similarities, which has been shown to take into account both syntactic and semantic similarities (Mikolov et al., 2013a). Thus, in the weighted language graph $\Omega_L(V, e)$, the weight function $e : (V \times V) \to \Re$ is defined by word-vector cosine similarities between pairs of words. Although word vectors are calculated based on co-occurrences of words within sliding windows, they are capable of attributing a reasonable degree of similarity to close words that do not co-occur.

Joint analysis of language graphs: By having word vector proximity as a measure of word similarity, we can represent each language as a joint similarity distribution of its words. Unlike the methods mentioned in section 1.1.3 which focused on network properties and did not consider a mapping function between nodes across various languages, we propose performing node alignment between different languages (Lardilleux and Lepage, 2009). Consequently, calculation of Jensen-Shannon divergence between unified similarity distributions of the languages can provide us with a measure of distance between languages.

Language collection: In this study we perform language comparison for fifty natural languages and twelve genetic language.

Natural languages: We extracted a collection of sentence-aligned parallel corpora from bible translations for fifty languages spanning a variety of language families including Indo-European (Germanic, Italic, Slavic, Indo-Iranian), Austronesian, Sino-Tibetan, Altaic, Uralic, Afro-Asiatic, etc. This set of languages is relatively large and diverse in comparison with the corpora that have been used in previous studies (Liu and Cong, 2013; Gao et al., 2014). We calculated the Jensen-Shannon divergence between joint similarity distributions for fifty language graphs consisting of 4,097 sets of aligned words in all these fifty languages. Using the mentioned divergence we performed cluster analysis of languages. Interestingly in many cases languages within the same family clustered together. In some cases, a lower degree of divergence from the source language despite belonging to different language families was indicative of a consistent translation.

Genetic languages: Nature uses certain languages to generate biological sequences such as DNA, RNA, and proteins. Biological organisms use sophisticated languages to convey information within and between cells, much like humans adopt languages to communicate (Yandell and Majoros, 2002; Searls, 2002). Inspired by this conceptual analogy, we use our languages comparison method for comparison of genetic languages in different organisms. Genome refers to a sequence of nucleotides containing our genetic information. Some parts of our genome are coded in a way that can be translated to proteins (exonic regions), while some regions cannot be translated into proteins (introns) (Saxonov et al., 2000). In this study, we perform language comparison of coding regions in 12 different species (4 plants, 6 animals, and two human subjects). Our language comparison method is able to assign a reasonable relative distance between species.

2   Methods

As we discussed in 1.1, we transfer the problem of finding a measure of distance between languages L and L' to finding the distance between their language graphs $\Omega_L(V, e)$ and $\Omega_{L'}(V', e')$.

Word Embedding: We define the edge weight function $e : (V \times V) \to \Re$ to be the cosine similarity between word vectors.

Alignment: When two languages have different words, in order to find a mapping between the words in V and V' we can perform statistical word alignment on parallel corpora.

Divergence Calculation: Calculating Jensen-Shannon divergence between joint similarity distributions of the languages can provide us with a notion of distance between languages.

Our language comparison method has three components. Firstly, we need to learn word vectors from large amounts of data in an unsupervised manner for both of the languages we are going to compare. Secondly, we need to find a mapping function for the words and finally we need to calculate the divergence between languages. In the following section we explain each step aligned with the experiment we perform on both natural languages and genetic languages.

2.1   Learning Word Embedding

Word embedding can be trained in various frameworks (e.g. non-negative matrix factorization and neural network methods (Mikolov et al., 2013c; Levy and Goldberg, 2014)). Neural network word embedding trained in the course of language modeling is shown to capture interesting syntactic and semantic regularities in the data (Mikolov et al., 2013c; Mikolov et al., 2013a). Such word embedding known as word vectors need to be trained from a large number of training examples, which are basically words and their corresponding contexts. In this project, in particular we use an implementation of the skip-gram neural network (Mikolov et al., 2013b).

In training word vector representations, the skip-gram neural network attempts to maximize the average probability of contexts for given words in the training data:

$$\operatorname*{argmax}_{v,v'} \frac{1}{N} \sum_{i=1}^{N} \sum_{-c \leq j \leq c, j \neq 0} \log p(w_{i+j}|w_i)$$

$$p(w_{i+j}|w_i) = \frac{\exp\left(v'^T_{w_{i+j}} v_{w_i}\right)}{\sum_{k=1}^{W} \exp\left(v'^T_{w_k} v_{w_i}\right)}, \tag{1}$$

where N is the length of the training, $2c$ is the window size we consider as the context, w_i is the center of the window, W is the number of words in the dictionary and v_w and v'_w are the n-dimensional word representation and context representation of word w, respectively. At the end of the training the average of v_w and v'_w will be considered as the word vector for w. The probability $p(w_{i+j}|w_i)$ is defined using a softmax function. In the implementation we use (Word2Vec) (Mikolov et al., 2013b) negative sampling has been utilized, which is considered as the state-of-the-art for training word vector representation.

2.1.1 Natural Languages Data

For the purpose of language classification we need parallel corpora that are translated into a large number of languages, so that we can find the alignments using statistical methods. Recently, a massive parallel corpus based on 100 translations of the Bible has been created in XML format (Christodouloupoulos and Steedman, 2015), which we choose as the database for this project. In order to make sure that we have a large enough corpus for learning word vectors, we pick the languages for which translations of both the Old Testament and the New Testament are available. From among those languages we pick the ones containing all the verses in the Hebrew version (which is the source language for most of the data) and finally we end up with almost 50 languages, containing 24,785 aligned verses. For Thai, Japanese, and Chinese we use the tokenized versions in

the database (Christodouloupoulos and Steedman, 2015). In addition, before feeding the skip-gram neural network we remove all punctuation.

In our experiment, we use the word2vec implementation of skip-gram (Mikolov et al., 2013b). We set the dimension of word vectors d to 100, and the window size c to 10 and we sub-sample the frequent words by the ratio $\frac{1}{10^3}$.

2.1.2 Genetic Languages Data

In order to compare the various genetic languages we use the IntronExon database that contains coding and non-coding regions of genomes for a number of organisms (Shepelev and Fedorov, 2006). From this database we extract a data-set of coding regions (CR) from 12 organisms consisting of 4 plants (arabidopsis, populus, moss, and rice), 6 animals (sea-urchin, chicken, cow, dog, mouse, and rat), and two human subjects. The number of coding regions we have in the training data for each organism is summarized in Table 1. The next step is splitting each sequence to a number of words. Since the genome is composed of the four DNA nucleotides A,T,G and C, if we split the sequences in the character level the language network would be very small. We thus split each sequence into n-grams ($n = 3, 4, 5, 6$), which is a common range of n-grams in bioinformatics(Ganapathiraju et al., 2002; Mantegna et al., 1995). As suggested by(Asgari and Mofrad, 2015) we split the sequence into non-overlapping n-grams, but we consider all possible ways of splitting for each sequence.

Organisms	# of CR	# of 3-grams
Arabidopsis	179824	42,618,288
Populus	131844	28,478,304
Moss	167999	38,471,771
Rice	129726	34,507,116
Sea-urchin	143457	27,974,115
Chicken	187761	34,735,785
Cow	196466	43,222,520
Dog	381147	70,512,195
Mouse	215274	34,874,388
Rat	190989	41,635,602
Human 1	319391	86,874,352
Human 2	303872	77,791,232

Table 1: The genome data-set for learning word vectors in different organisms. The number of coding regions and the total occurrences of 3-grams are presented. Clearly, the total number of all n-grams (n=3,4,5,6) is almost the same.

We train the word vectors for each setting of n-grams and organisms separately, again using skip-gram neural network implementation (Mikolov et al., 2013b). We set the dimension of word vectors d to 100, and window size of c to 40. In addition, we sub-sample the frequent words by the ratio 10^-3.

2.2 Word Alignment

The next step is to find a mapping between the nodes in $\Omega_L(V, e)$ and $\Omega_{L'}(V', e')$. Obviously in case of quantitative comparison of styles within the same language we do not need to find an alignment between the nodes in V and V'. However, when we are comparing two distinct languages we need to find a mapping from the words in language L to the words in language L'.

2.2.1 Word Alignment for Natural Languages

As we mentioned in section 2.1.1, our parallel corpora contain texts in fifty languages from a variety of language families. We decided to use statistical word alignments because we already have parallel corpora for these languages and therefore performing statistical alignment is straightforward. In addition, using statistical alignment we hope to see evidences of consistent/inconsistent translations.

We use an implementation of Anymalign (Lardilleux and Lepage, 2009), which is designed to extract high quality word alignments from sentence-aligned multilingual parallel corpora. Although Anymalign is capable of performing alignments in several languages at the same time, our empirical observation was that performing alignments for all languages against a single language and then finding the global alignment through that alignment is faster and results in better alignments. We thus align all translations with the Hebrew version. To ensure the quality of alignments we apply a high threshold on the score of alignments. In a final step, we combine the results and end up with a set of 4,097 multilingual alignments. Hence we have a mapping from any of the 4,097 words in one language to one in any other given language, where the Hebrew words are unique, but not necessarily the others.

2.2.2 Genetic Languages Alignment

In genetic language comparison, since the n-grams are generated from the same nucleotides (A,T,C,G), no alignment is needed and V would be the same as V'.

2.3 Calculation of Language Divergence

In section 2.1 we explained how to make language graphs $\Omega_L(V, e)$ and $\Omega_{L'}(V', e')$. Then in section 2.2 we proposed a statistical alignment method to find the mapping function between the nodes in V and V'. Having achieved the mapping between the words in V and the words in V', the next step is comparison of e and e'.

In comparing language graphs what is more crucial is the *relative* similarities of words. Intuitively we know that the relative similarities of words vary in different languages due to syntactic and semantic differences. Hence, we decided to use the divergence between relative similarities of words as a heuristic measure of the distance between two languages. To do so, firstly we normalize the relative word vector similarities within each language. Then, knowing the mapping between words in V and V' we unify the coordinates of the normalized similarity distributions. Finally, we calculate the Jensen-Shannon divergence between the normalized and unified similarity distributions of two languages:

$$D_{L,L'} = JSD(\hat{e}, \hat{e}'),$$

where $\hat{e}$ and $\hat{e}'$ are normalized and unified similarity distributions of word pairs in $\Omega_L(V, e)$ and $\Omega_{L'}(V', e')$ respectively.

2.3.1 Natural Languages Graphs

For the purpose of language classification we need to find pairwise distances between all of the fifty languages we have in our corpora. Using the mapping function obtained from statistical alignments of Bible translations, we produce the normalized and unified similarity distributions of word pairs $\hat{e^{(k)}}$ for language $L^{(k)}$. Therefore to compute the quantitative distance between two languages $L^{(i)}$ and $L^{(j)}$ we calculate $D_{L_i, L_j} = JSD(\hat{e^{(i)}}, \hat{e^{(j)}})$.

Consequently, we calculate a quantitative distance between each pair of languages. In a final step, for visualization purposes, we perform Unweighted Pair Group Method with Arithmetic Mean (UPGMA) hierarchical clustering on the pairwise distance matrix of languages (Johnson, 1967).

2.3.2 Genetic Languages Graphs

The same approach as carried out for natural languages is applied to genetic languages corpora. Pairwise distances of genetic languages were calculated using Jensen-Shannon divergence between normalized and unified similarity distributions of word pairs for each pair of languages.

We calculate the pairwise distance matrix of languages for each n-gram separately to verify which length of DNA segment is more discriminative between different species.

3   Results

3.1   Classification of Natural Languages

The result of the UPGMA hierarchical clustering of languages is shown in Figure 1. As shown in this figure, many languages are clustered together according to their family and sub-family. Many Indo-European languages (shown in green) and Austronesian languages (shown in pink) are within a close proximity. Even the proximity between languages within a sub-family are preserved with our measure of language distance. For instance, Romanian, Spanish, French, Italian, and Portuguese, all of which belong to the Italic sub-family of Indo-European languages, are in the same cluster. Similarly, the Austronesian langauges Cebuano, Tagalog, and Maori as well as Malagasy and Indonesian are grouped together.

Although the clustering based on word embedding language divergence matches the genetic/typological classification of languages in many cases, for some pairs of languages their distance in the clustering does not make any genetic or topological sense. For instance, we expected Arabic and Somali as Afro-Asiatic languages to be within a close proximity with Hebrew. However, Hebrew is matched with Norwegian, a Germanic Indo-European language. After further investigations and comparing word neighbors for several cases in these languages, it turns out that the Norwegian bible translation highly matches Hebrew because of being a consistent and high-quality translation. In this translation, synonym were not used interchangeably and language usage stays more faithful to the structure of the Hebrew text.

3.1.1   Divergence between Genetic Languages

The pairwise distance matrix of the twelve genetic languages for n-grams ($n = 3, 4, 5, 6$) is shown in Figure 2. Our results confirm that evolutionarily closer species have a reasonably higher level of proximity in their language models. We can observe in Figure 2, that as we increase the number of n-grams the distinction between animal/human genome and plant genome increases.

4   Conclusion

In this paper, we proposed Word Embedding Language Divergence (WELD) as a new heuristic measure of distance between languages. Consequently we performed language comparison for fifty natural languages and twelve genetic languages. Our natural language dataset was a collection of sentence-aligned parallel corpora from bible translations for fifty languages spanning a variety of language families. We calculated our word embedding language divergence for 4,097 sets of aligned words in all these fifty languages. Using the mentioned divergence we performed cluster analysis of languages.

The corpora for all of the languages but one consisted of translated text instead of original text in those languages. This means many of the potential relations between words such as collocations and culturally influenced semantic connotations did not have the full chance to contribute to the measured language distances. This can potentially make it harder for the algorithm to detect related languages. In spite of this, however in many cases languages within the same family/sub-family clustered together. In some cases, a lower degree of divergence from the source language despite belonging to different language families was indicative of a consistent translation. This suggests that this method can be a step toward defining a quantitative measure of similarity between languages, with applications in languages classification, genres identification, dialect identification, and evaluation of translations.

In addition to the natural language data-set, we performed language comparison of n-grams in coding regions of the genome in 12 different species (4 plants, 6 animals, and two human subjects). Our language comparison method confirmed that evolutionarily closer species are closer in terms of genetic language models. Interestingly, as we increase the number of n-grams the distinction between genetic language in animals/human versus plants increases. This can be regarded as indicative of a high-level diversity between the genetic languages in plants versus animals.

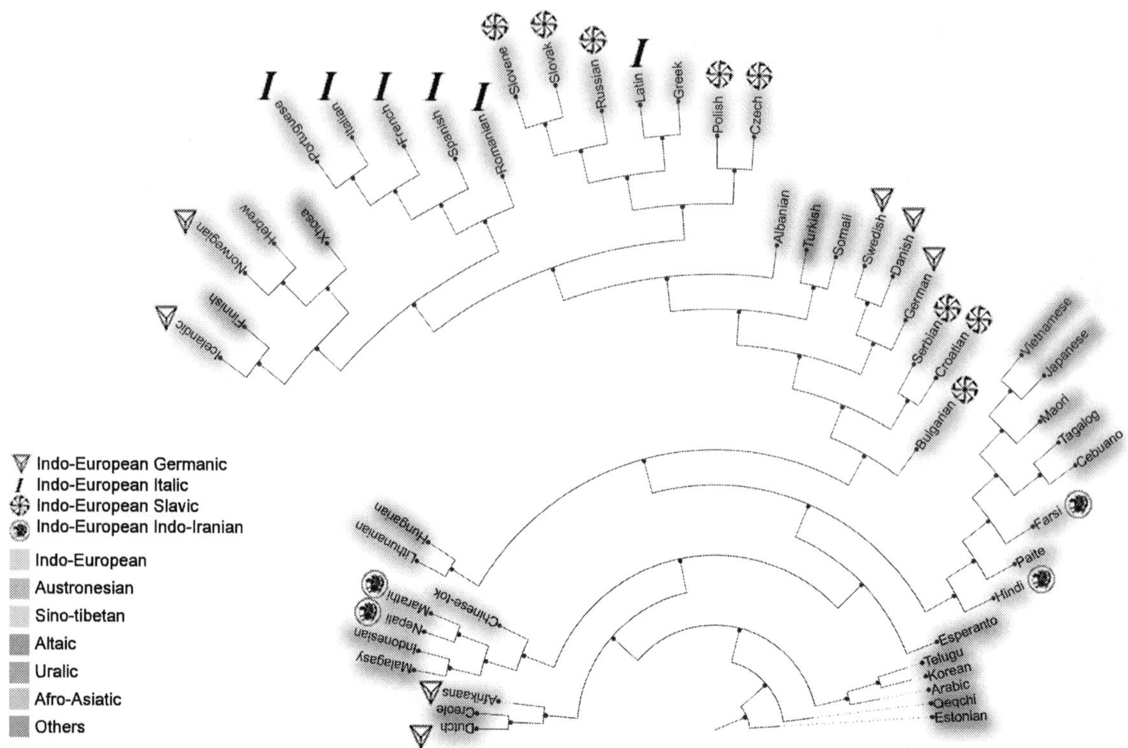

Figure 1: Hierarchical clustering of fifty natural languages according to divergence of joint distance distribution of 4097 aligned words in bible parallel corpora. Subsequently we use colors to show the ground-truth about family of languages. For Indo-European languages we use different symbols to distinguish various sub-families of Indo-European languages. We observe that the obtained clustering reasonably discriminates between various families and subfamilies.

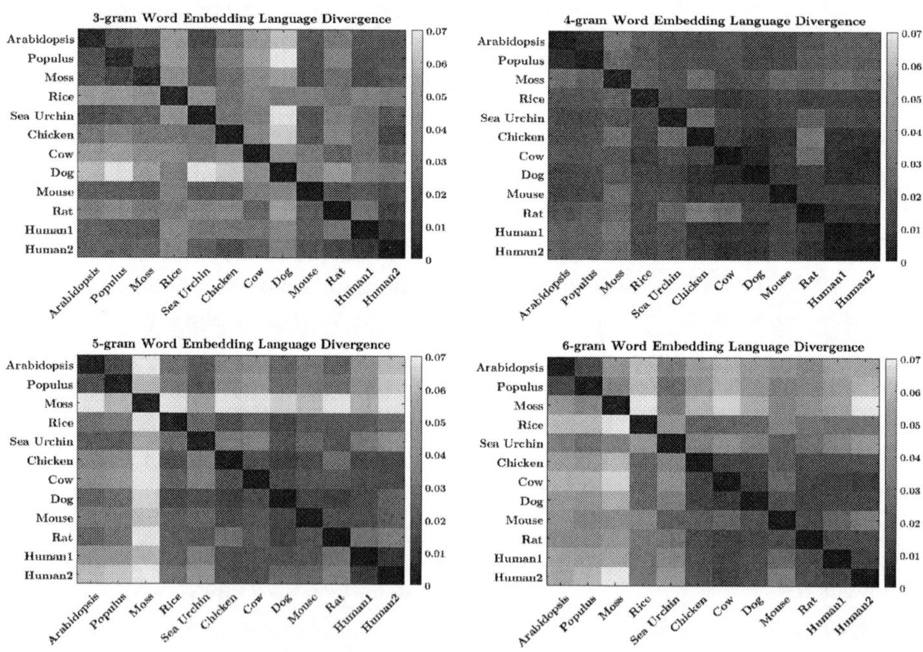

Figure 2: Visualization of word embedding language divergence in twelve different genomes belonging to 12 organisms for various n-gram segments. Our results indicate that evolutionarily closer species have higher proximity in the syntax and semantics of their genomes.

Acknowledgments

Fruitful discussions with David Bamman, Meshkat Ahmadi, and Mohsen Mahdavi are gratefully acknowledged.

References

Ehsaneddin Asgari and Mohammad RK Mofrad. 2015. Continuous distributed representation of biological sequences for deep proteomics and genomics. *PloS one*, 10(11):e0141287.

Taylor Berg-Kirkpatrick and Dan Klein. 2010. Phylogenetic grammar induction. In *Proceedings of the 48th Annual Meeting of the Association for Computational Linguistics*, pages 1288–1297. Association for Computational Linguistics.

David M Blei. 2012. Probabilistic topic models. *Communications of the ACM*, 55(4):77–84.

Alexandre Bouchard-Côté, David Hall, Thomas L Griffiths, and Dan Klein. 2013. Automated reconstruction of ancient languages using probabilistic models of sound change. *Proceedings of the National Academy of Sciences*, 110(11):4224–4229.

Christos Christodouloupoulos and Mark Steedman. 2015. A massively parallel corpus: the bible in 100 languages. *Language resources and evaluation*, 49(2):375–395.

Alina Maria Ciobanu and Liviu P. Dinu. 2014. An etymological approach to cross-language orthographic similarity. application on romanian. In *Proceedings of the 2014 Conference on Empirical Methods in Natural Language Processing (EMNLP)*, pages 1047–1058, Doha, Qatar, October. Association for Computational Linguistics.

Ronan Collobert and Jason Weston. 2008. A unified architecture for natural language processing: Deep neural networks with multitask learning. In *Proceedings of the 25th international conference on Machine learning*, pages 160–167. ACM.

Ronan Collobert, Jason Weston, Léon Bottou, Michael Karlen, Koray Kavukcuoglu, and Pavel Kuksa. 2011. Natural language processing (almost) from scratch. *The Journal of Machine Learning Research*, 12:2493–2537.

Jin Cong and Haitao Liu. 2014. Approaching human language with complex networks. *Physics of life reviews*, 11(4):598–618.

Luciano da Fontoura Costa, Osvaldo N Oliveira Jr, Gonzalo Travieso, Francisco Aparecido Rodrigues, Paulino Ribeiro Villas Boas, Lucas Antiqueira, Matheus Palhares Viana, and Luis Enrique Correa Rocha. 2011. Analyzing and modeling real-world phenomena with complex networks: a survey of applications. *Advances in Physics*, 60(3):329–412.

John Rupert Firth. 1975. *Modes of meaning*. College Division of Bobbs-Merrill Company.

Alexander Fraser and Daniel Marcu. 2007. Measuring word alignment quality for statistical machine translation. *Computational Linguistics*, 33(3):293–303.

Madhavi Ganapathiraju, Deborah Weisser, Roni Rosenfeld, Jaime Carbonell, Raj Reddy, and Judith Klein-Seetharaman. 2002. Comparative n-gram analysis of whole-genome protein sequences. In *Proceedings of the second international conference on Human Language Technology Research*, pages 76–81. Morgan Kaufmann Publishers Inc.

Yuyang Gao, Wei Liang, Yuming Shi, and Qiuling Huang. 2014. Comparison of directed and weighted co-occurrence networks of six languages. *Physica A: Statistical Mechanics and its Applications*, 393:579–589.

Xavier Glorot, Antoine Bordes, and Yoshua Bengio. 2011. Domain adaptation for large-scale sentiment classification: A deep learning approach. In *Proceedings of the 28th International Conference on Machine Learning (ICML-11)*, pages 513–520.

David Hall and Dan Klein. 2010. Finding cognate groups using phylogenies. In *Proceedings of the 48th Annual Meeting of the Association for Computational Linguistics*, pages 1030–1039. Association for Computational Linguistics.

Lushan Han, Tim Finin, Paul McNamee, Akanksha Joshi, and Yelena Yesha. 2013. Improving word similarity by augmenting pmi with estimates of word polysemy. *Knowledge and Data Engineering, IEEE Transactions on*, 25(6):1307–1322.

Geoffrey E Hinton. 1984. Distributed representations. *Computer Science Department, Carnegie Mellon University*.

Ramon Ferrer i Cancho and Richard V Solé. 2001. The small world of human language. *Proceedings of the Royal Society of London B: Biological Sciences*, 268(1482):2261–2265.

Stephen C Johnson. 1967. Hierarchical clustering schemes. *Psychometrika*, 32(3):241–254.

Jiři Krámský. 1959. A quantitative typology of languages. *Language and speech*, 2(2):72–85.

Alfred L Kroeber and C Douglas Chrétien. 1937. Quantitative classification of indo-european languages. *Language*, 13(2):83–103.

Vivek Kulkarni, Rami Al-Rfou, Bryan Perozzi, and Steven Skiena. 2015. Statistically significant detection of linguistic change. In *Proceedings of the 24th International Conference on World Wide Web*, pages 625–635. International World Wide Web Conferences Steering Committee.

Adrien Lardilleux and Yves Lepage. 2009. Sampling-based multilingual alignment. In *Recent Advances in Natural Language Processing*, pages 214–218.

Omer Levy and Yoav Goldberg. 2014. Neural word embedding as implicit matrix factorization. In *Advances in Neural Information Processing Systems*, pages 2177–2185.

HaiTao Liu and Jin Cong. 2013. Language clustering with word co-occurrence networks based on parallel texts. *Chinese Science Bulletin*, 58(10):1139–1144.

RN Mantegna, SV Buldyrev, AL Goldberger, S Havlin, C-K Peng, M Simons, and HE Stanley. 1995. Systematic analysis of coding and noncoding dna sequences using methods of statistical linguistics. *Physical Review E*, 52(3):2939.

M Marjorie and Janie Rees-Miller. 2001. Language in social contexts. *Contemporary Linguistics*, pages 537–590.

April McMahon and Robert McMahon. 2003. Finding families: quantitative methods in language classification. *Transactions of the Philological Society*, 101(1):7–55.

Tomas Mikolov, Kai Chen, Greg Corrado, and Jeffrey Dean. 2013a. Efficient estimation of word representations in vector space. *arXiv preprint arXiv:1301.3781*.

Tomas Mikolov, Ilya Sutskever, Kai Chen, Greg S Corrado, and Jeff Dean. 2013b. Distributed representations of words and phrases and their compositionality. In *Advances in neural information processing systems*, pages 3111–3119.

Tomas Mikolov, Wen-tau Yih, and Geoffrey Zweig. 2013c. Linguistic regularities in continuous space word representations. In *HLT-NAACL*, pages 746–751.

George A Miller. 1995. Wordnet: a lexical database for english. *Communications of the ACM*, 38(11):39–41.

Saif Mohammad and Graeme Hirst. 2006. Distributional measures of concept-distance: A task-oriented evaluation. In *Proceedings of the 2006 Conference on Empirical Methods in Natural Language Processing*, pages 35–43. Association for Computational Linguistics.

Franz Josef Och and Hermann Ney. 2003. A systematic comparison of various statistical alignment models. *Computational linguistics*, 29(1):19–51.

FJ Och. 2003. Giza++ software.

Philip Resnik. 1999. Semantic similarity in a taxonomy: An information-based measure and its application to problems of ambiguity in natural language. *J. Artif. Intell. Res.(JAIR)*, 11:95–130.

CR Sankaran, AD Taskar, and PC Ganeshsundaram. 1950. Quantitative classification of languages. *Bulletin of the Deccan College Research Institute*, pages 85–111.

Serge Saxonov, Iraj Daizadeh, Alexei Fedorov, and Walter Gilbert. 2000. Eid: the exon–intron databasean exhaustive database of protein-coding intron-containing genes. *Nucleic acids research*, 28(1):185–190.

Holger Schwenk. 2007. Continuous space language models. *Computer Speech & Language*, 21(3):492–518.

David B Searls. 2002. The language of genes. *Nature*, 420(6912):211–217.

Valery Shepelev and Alexei Fedorov. 2006. Advances in the exon–intron database (eid). *Briefings in bioinformatics*, 7(2):178–185.

Andrew DM Smith. 2016. Dynamic models of language evolution: The linguistic perspective.

Efstathios Stamatatos, Nikos Fakotakis, and George Kokkinakis. 2000. Text genre detection using common word frequencies. In *Proceedings of the 18th conference on Computational linguistics-Volume 2*, pages 808–814. Association for Computational Linguistics.

Peter D Turney, Patrick Pantel, et al. 2010. From frequency to meaning: Vector space models of semantics. *Journal of artificial intelligence research*, 37(1):141–188.

Wei Xu, Xin Liu, and Yihong Gong. 2003. Document clustering based on non-negative matrix factorization. In *Proceedings of the 26th annual international ACM SIGIR conference on Research and development in informaion retrieval*, pages 267–273. ACM.

Mark D Yandell and William H Majoros. 2002. Genomics and natural language processing. *Nature Reviews Genetics*, 3(8):601–610.